"For anyone interested in creating their own TV series in the growing world of Internet video, this is the one book you need to get started."
— John Churchman, publisher: *School Video News*

"Ross Brown's book opens up creativity to amazing possibilities. Read this book and then take the leap into telling stories in a different way, through a different medium – you may very well surprise yourself."
— Matthew Terry, filmmaker/screenwriter/teacher, columnist: *www.hollywoodlitsales.com*

"Ross Brown's book is chock full of helpful advice for young filmmakers, starting with the premise that the Internet offers a level playing field for just about anyone with enough ambition and fresh ideas to make a webisode. Based on his years of experience writing for network television, he analyzes and breaks down the components of what makes a successful show in this new cutting-edge medium. Ross Brown offers common sense guidance to the DIY filmmaker as well as to the seasoned pro who are seeking new outlets for their creative talents."
— Scott Arundale, Assistant Professor – Dodge College of Film and Media Arts

"An experienced TV showrunner and esteemed professor, Ross Brown has written a practical, step-by-step guide to writing, producing, directing, editing, and distributing a new breed of TV series for the 21st century. With insight and candor, *Byte-Sized Television* blazes a trail into the exciting frontier of New Media."
— Neil Landau, screenwriter/producer, Professor – UCLA School of Film, Television, and Digital Media, author: *101 Things I Learned in Film School*

"*Byte-Sized Television* takes you inside the creative process and teaches you how to think and work like a pro. Outstanding guidance, advice and inspiration for anyone who wants to make a web series."
— Joel Surnow, Emmy-winning co-creator and executive producer of *24*

"This superb primer by Ross Brown covers every step of development and production with both humor and serious professionalism. This kind of priceless lesson could only come from the real-life experiences of a seasoned writer/producer like Brown, and it fills every page of *Byte-Sized Television*. If you want a real shot at making it big in the world of web series, don't just read this book... digest it, absorb it, then get to work and make it happen!"
— Adam Wolman, consultant, Microflix; development consultant, HBO Digital; exec consultant, Disney/ABC TV Group; VP, Original Series, MTV; director, Comedy, ABC; exec producer of ABC/TTV's Micro-Mini Series.

"Ross Brown has captured the uncaptureable: Identifying the elements of successful (and not-so-successful) web series. He walks readers through every step of making their own *Sanctuary* or *We Need Girlfriends*, from creating a fresh concept, to buying the right cameras and editing equipment."

— Chad Gervich, writer/producer: *Foody Call, Wipeout, Speeders, Reality Binge*; author: *Small Screen, Big Picture: A Writer's Guide to the TV Business*

"Here are the four essentials to making a webisode: a camera, performers, editing, and this book. That's all you need to get started."

— Frank Chindamo, President and Chief Creative Officer of *FunLittleMovies .com*

BYTE-SIZED
TELEVISION

CREATE YOUR OWN TV SERIES FOR THE INTERNET

ROSS BROWN

MICHAEL WIESE PRODUCTIONS

Published by Michael Wiese Productions
12400 Ventura Blvd. #1111
Studio City, CA 91604
(818) 379-8799, (818) 986-3408 (FAX)
mw@mwp.com
www.mwp.com

Cover design by Johnny Ink. www.johnnyink.com
Interior design by William Morosi
Printed by McNaughton & Gunn

Manufactured in the United States of America

Library of Congress Cataloging-in-Publication Data

Brown, Ross, 1954-
 Byte-sized television : create your own tv series for the Internet / Ross Brown.
    p. cm.
 ISBN 978-1-932907-86-5
1. Television authorship. 2. Internet television. I. Title.
 PN1992.7.B76 2011
 808'.066791--dc22

                                   2010030970

TABLE OF CONTENTS

ACKNOWLEDGMENTS

First thanks go to my colleagues at the Dodge College of Film and Media Arts at Chapman University. In particular I would like to thank Dean Bob Bassett and Media Arts Division Chair Janell Shearer for their support and guidance of both my teaching and the writing of this book. I would also like to thank Professor James Gardner for suggesting that I write this book, Professor Gil Bettman for introducing me to my publishers, Ken Lee and Michael Wiese, and Deszo Magyar and Ron Friedman for helping me arrange some key interviews for this book.

I would also like to thank my students, particularly those who have taken my Byte-Sized Television courses. You inspire me with your creativity, challenge me with your questions, force me to think deeply, and remind me every day that life is about learning.

Thanks also to my writing colleagues who have shared so many insights about craft with me over the years, especially Bruce Watson, Neil Landau and Deborah Brevoort.

Eternal thanks, gratitude and love to my daughters Alexis and Rachel for their support, encouragement and the joy they bring to my life. And most of all, my deepest thanks, gratitude and love to my wife Wendy for the infinite gifts you've given me over the years — love, encouragement, wisdom, space, passion, compassion, joy, heart, and laughter.

WHAT'S THIS BOOK ABOUT AND WHO IS IT FOR?

Every producer, network, studio and cable channel in Hollywood is spending thousands of hours and millions of dollars trying to figure out how to connect with the YouTube audience and make a hit Internet TV series. And it's a solid bet that this breakout short-form hit will come not from Hollywood, but from the mind of someone outside the established media power structure. Someone like you.

That's not to say that this trailblazer will necessarily be a rank amateur. Maybe he'll be a writer who's been trying to break into network television but hasn't succeeded yet. Or maybe she'll be writing for another medium that Hollywood or the Internet suddenly discovers (can you say Diablo Cody?). Or maybe it will be a veteran writer who has been churning out bland sitcoms for decades, someone seen as over the hill, someone who throws caution to the wind and creates something totally new and original because the traditional doors to employment are now slammed in his face (can you say Marc Cherry, creator of *Desperate Housewives*?). Or maybe it will be someone now in film school, or even in high school, who came of age during the digital era, thinks visually, and who intuitively knows what her peers crave in the way of short video entertainment, in part because watching short videos is a normal part of their daily experience.

The point is that everybody knows there is a hit webisode series lurking on the horizon, but nobody knows where it will come from. They only know that, sooner or later, there will be a breakthrough smash hit in the Internet TV realm. So it might as well come from YOU!

Webisodes are the Wild West of Hollywood, a vast expanse of territory with unlimited potential just begging to be explored and mined. The territory is open to anyone with a dream and the moxie to follow that dream. You may strike oil, or find gold — or you may end up with a handful of dust. Either way, the journey will be exciting and rewarding for its own sake.

But before you head out on this quest to create your own Internet TV series, you need a few vital supplies: some basic equipment and know-how, a workable series premise, a pilot script, a shooting budget and a shot list. In short — you need a plan.

This book is designed to help you draw up that plan, step by step. You are HERE. Somewhere out THERE on the Internet is a place for a television series created by YOU. This book is the map that can lead you from where you are now — a person with a lot of creative ideas in their head but no clear idea how to turn those buzzing ideas into reality — to THERE, the creator of your own unique and exciting TV series designed for the Web.

I know it can be done because my students at the Dodge College of Film and Media Arts at Chapman University have been creating innovative, entertaining web series for the past two years. You know it can be done because you've surfed the Net, seen the good, the bad and the ugly out there, and said — "I can do better than that."

You're absolutely right. You can do better than most of what's out there. And you don't need a million-dollar budget or a Hollywood studio full of equipment to do it. Anyone with a digital camcorder and an average computer has all the equipment he needs right now to make a webisode series.

What you don't have, most likely, is exposure to the thought process involved in taking a raw idea for a short-form TV show and shaping that vague notion into a clear premise, defined characters, a story to introduce those characters in an engaging way, and the professional know-how to take that story through all phases of production and end up with a polished and marketable pilot episode.

Make no mistake: it won't be easy. You can't just slap together some half-baked notion, grab a camcorder and point it randomly at things that strike you as interesting or funny. That's just video masturbation. All you end up with, as Mike Judge suggests in his film *Idiocracy*, is a show called *"Ow! My balls!"*

You may also need some help understanding the best way to market your web TV series — that is, the best way to let the audience know what you've created and get them interested in watching your show. Simply posting something on YouTube is not enough. The Internet is a cacophony of voices screaming, "Watch me! Watch me!" You have to find ways to make your voice, and your web series, stand out from the crowd. A great series concept and superior execution are only good first steps. To get eyeballs to your show, however, you'll need to apply a little Web 2.0 marketing savvy.

But if you have a sincere desire to create quality comedy or drama in an episodic form for the Internet, and to commit the time and energy necessary to market your work, then read on. As my students have taught me over and over again, there is an unlimited and untapped supply of amazing, fresh, compelling creative ideas out there, begging to find their way to the screen. This book will help you to tap into that vast reservoir of creativity and give your ideas form, shape and professional quality. It's the ultimate win-win situation: you get a shot at creating a hit TV show for the Internet, and we, the millions of daily consumers of short-form Internet videos, get a shot at watching something more compelling than *"Ow! My balls!"*

For the sake of all our days and nights, read on and create something fantastic for all of us to watch.

CHAPTER ONE
WHAT IS A WEBISODE?

Simply put, a "webisode" is an episode of a television series designed for distribution over the Internet. It can be comedy like *General Elevator* (on National Banana and YouTube) or *Gaytown* (on Crackle) or compelling drama like *quarterlife* (at *quarterlife.com*). It can be live action or animated, fiction, or reality-based like cable network Lifetime's original online series *Gift Intervention* (at *mylifetime.com*). It can be a high-budget, intricately filmed sci-fi extravaganza with dazzling special effects like *Sanctuary* (at *sanctuaryforall.com*) that costs $4.3 million, or approximately $32,000 per minute — arguably the most ambitious film project to date designed for direct release over the Internet. Or it can be as low-tech as a static webcam shot in front of a convenient and free background like your own bedroom (see any number of shows on YouTube). And as far as length, it can be whatever you choose — from 10 seconds to however long you can hold the audience's attention.

The key word is *series*. A webisode (or web episode) is an individual installment of an ongoing premise with recurring characters. A single, stand-alone short video — say of the hilarious things your cat did after she lapped up your Jack Daniels on the rocks — is NOT a webisode. Neither is that brilliant spoof of *Sex And The City* you shot at your grandmother's retirement home — unless you shot a series of short *SATC* spoofs with grandma and her horny pals, in which case we should take the Jack Daniels away from you and grandma and give it back to your cat.

A Brief History Of Short Episodic Video On The Web

In the Mel Brooks movie *History Of The World, Part I*, Moses (played by Brooks) descends from a mountain lugging three stone tablets chiseled with 15 commandments from God — until Moses trips and drops one of the holy tablets, shattering it beyond recognition. Thinking quickly, he declares, "I bring you ten... *TEN* commandments!" Five sacred commandments smashed into a pile of rubble just like that. Who knows what wisdom was lost? Maybe the missing commandments said things like *Thou shalt not wear spandex after age 40* or *Covet not thy neighbor's iPhone for he is a tech dunce and can't work it anyway*. Your guess is as good as mine. But whatever moral pearls turned to dust in that moment, I'm pretty sure one of the lost commandments was not *Thou shalt only make TV shows in increments of 30 or 60 minutes*.

Since the dawn of the television age in the 1940s, broadcasters have been prisoners of the clock, confined to airing shows on the hour and half hour so viewers would know when and where to find them. But the digital revolution and the Internet have changed all that. More and more, television and visual entertainment in general are part of an on-demand world. Audiences can now watch what they want when they want, which, in turn, means that shows no longer have to be packaged in 30- or 60-minute installments.

It's a revolution that has fed on itself. Free from the tyranny of the 30/60 paradigm, short-form video content in all shapes and sizes has exploded on the Web. Maybe a show is two minutes and thirty-seven seconds long one time, maybe it runs six minutes and forty-one seconds the next. Each episode can be however long it deserves to be.

Audiences, in turn, have responded by growing their viewing habits. Where you used to need at least a half-hour to watch your favorite comedy, now you might be able to catch two or three episodes of it in less than fifteen minutes. Office workers now schedule "video breaks' rather than coffee breaks, boosting their energy and outlook by guzzling down a few short comedy videos for free instead of a double espresso caramel latte for five bucks. Or maybe you choose to watch a few webisodes on the bus or the train on your laptop or mobile device.

Never before have viewers had so many choices. And never before have creators had so much latitude on the length and type of content they can make.

In truth, short-form episodic film series have been around since well before the days of television, some even coming during the silent movie era. Charlie Chaplin, Harold Lloyd and Buster Keaton all created "one reelers" — popular early predecessors to today's web series, shot on film and exhibited in theaters alongside the newsreel and the feature presentation. In the animated realm, the *Looney Tunes* shorts come to mind. But the equipment and processing necessary to make even a two-minute film back then were so expensive that only professionals could afford to make these shorts. And even if an amateur had the funds and imagination to produce a clever short film, distribution was entirely controlled by the major Hollywood studios, who owned the theaters and who had no intention of allowing the competition to cut into their lucrative monopoly.

The advent of lightweight and relatively affordable personal camcorders by the early 1980s made it possible for millions to shoot their own videos. But most of these home videos were unedited, handheld footage of family vacations or children's birthday parties, usually narrated by Dad or Uncle Johnny: "Here we are at little Billy's second birthday party... here's Billy eating cake... here he is opening his presents... and here's little Billy pulling down his pants and relieving himself in the garden." As much as you (and years later, Big Billy) wish Dad had done a little judicious cutting, editing equipment and technology was still bulky and

Global media giant Sony Pictures Entertainment jumped in, creating a site called Grouper (now known as Crackle), "a multi-platform video entertainment network and studio that distributes the hottest emerging talent on the Web and beyond."

Disney launched Stage 9 Digital Media, a division dedicated to generating original online-only content. It debuted with a series called *Squeegees*, about window washers, created by a Los Angeles group known as Handsome Donkey.

Traditional broadcast networks like ABC, CBS and NBC, which at first cursed Internet video as the enemy (just as the major movie studios had cursed broadcast television as the enemy in the early days of TV), quickly realized Internet video was here to stay and that they needed to be part of it. They made full episodes of their shows available online and soon discovered that, rather than decreasing their overall audience, Internet availability of series expanded their reach. They also created original short-form webisodes for shows like *The Office* and *24*.

Established filmmakers loved the creative spirit of Internet video and dove into the webisode pool as well (though they stuck to using their real names instead of cool monikers like Big Fantastic and Handsome Donkey). Oscar-winning directors Joel and Ethan Coen (*No Country For Old Men, Fargo, The Big Lebowski*) committed to produce short features for 60Frames, a company run by former UTA Online head Brent Weinstein, with an ambitious production slate. *Charlie's Angels* director McG was hired by Warner Bros. to create a series called *Sorority Forever* for TheWB.com. Will Ferrell and other established stars contribute Internet videos to a site called Funny Or Die. Successful writer/producer/director Jerry Zucker (*Airplane!, The Naked Gun* movie series, *Ghost*) went so far as to form a new company, National Banana, with a sound stage and postproduction facilities and staff dedicated to creating online content.

Though A-list players were storming the Internet video world in droves, Hollywood also recognized that this new form demanded a new reservoir of creative inspiration and energy. Major Hollywood talent agencies like CAA and UTA formed divisions dedicated to finding new Internet talent, both in front of and behind the camera. These new agency divisions also sought to develop online opportunities for established mainstream clients who wanted to work in this exciting new realm.

Suddenly, once obscure guerilla video artists like Big Fantastic were in hot demand. Well-financed media mogul Michael Eisner, former CEO of The Walt Disney Company, hired Big Fantastic to create a web series called *Prom Queen*, which became a major hit, racking up more than 20 million views in short order. Eisner then upped the ante and hired Big Fantastic to shoot 50 two-minute episodes of *Foreign Body*, a medical thriller tied to the launch of a book by the same name by bestselling author Robin Cook.

For advertisers, who had long relied on television to provide the precious eyeballs they needed, the new Internet video culture presented a variety of problems. Not only were fewer people watching network television, but those who did were now armed with TiVo and other recording devices that allowed them to skip the commercials entirely. Advertisers quickly realized they needed to take the lemons they'd been handed and somehow make lemonade. Rather than merely placing the same old ads in this new entertainment arena, advertisers seized the opportunity and made new short-form content of their own that married their sales message *with* entertainment. Consumer giant Unilever promoted its new spray bottle version of I Can't Believe It's Not Butter through webisodes of a series called *Sprays Of Her Life*, a parody of soap operas with the slogan, "Romance. Passion. Deception. Vegetables. Watch things heat up when the refrigerator lights go down!" Anheuser Busch ponied up $30-million to create BudTV.com, a video site that promoted brands like Budweiser not only through product ads but by hosting original, non-advertising entertainment content aimed at their target audience produced by Internet-eager talent like Kevin Spacey, Matt Damon and Ben Affleck.

In the old network television advertising paradigm, advertisers looked for shows whose audience included the advertiser's target consumer group and bought 30-second spots on the show, hoping against the odds that the audience would stick around for the commercial message instead of muting the set, raiding the fridge, or taking a bathroom break. But in this new, short-form Internet video world, advertisers could design the entertainment to appeal to their consumers and embed their advertising message seamlessly into the entertainment itself.

It was a brave new world for everyone, Hollywood hotshots and newcomers alike. Nobody knew exactly what the Internet video future would look like, but everyone wanted to be a part of it.

What's Out There Now — Amateur And Professional

Trying to comprehensively catalogue every webisode series on the Internet is a bit like trying to count the number of popcorn kernels in the big bin at the multiplex. You'll never get the job done because fresh new nuggets pop out of the machine faster than you can count. Before I finish typing this sentence, someone, somewhere, will post a new Internet-based TV series. On the Internet, time is measured not in months or years, but in nanoseconds.

Still, as an aspiring content creator, it's vital that you survey the territory to get a basic sense of the existing landscape and scope of offerings. Start with the video segments of large Internet giants — YouTube, Yahoo! Video, Google Video, AOL Video, MSN Video, MySpace, and Facebook. Then explore sites featuring proprietary, professionally created content like Crackle and Funny Or Die. Finally, surf a variety of video-hosting sites that feature user-generated content. You'll inevitably have to wade through a sludge pile of things that don't appeal to you, but you'll also more than likely be inspired by some of what you see and find some favorite new short-form shows.

Here is a brief overview of some of the major sites, in alphabetical order:

Atom uploads — A video uploading and sharing service from AtomFilms, a division of MTV.

Blip.tv — Highly rated by *PC World*, this site syndicates its content with other major sites like AOL Video, Yahoo! Video, MSN Video, Twitter, Flickr, MySpace, Facebook, etc., so you'll be reaching many audiences just by posting on this one site.

Break.com — Creates and posts broad humor, both stand-alone and series, that targets an 18- to 34-year-old male audience.

Brightcove — This site allows you to establish your own Internet TV station, so it's a good choice for creators of multiple web series. Like Blip.tv, it syndicates with other major players, plus it offers opportunities to share ad revenue.

Crackle — Formerly known as Grouper, bills itself as being all about "launching tomorrow's stars today." The site is funded by Sony Pictures Entertainment and features a wide range of content.

FlickLife — A privately owned company based in Columbus, Ohio, this site offers free uploads and revenue sharing.

Fun Little Movies — Award-winning site that specializes in distributing content on mobile devices like smart phones.

Go Fish — A family-oriented site that targets kids, teens and their moms, a market they estimate at more than 70 million Internet users.

Jumpcut — Acquired by Yahoo! in 2006, this online creative community features a unique "Remix" button that allows you to test your editing and directing skills by taking someone else's video and recutting it into your own version.

Metacafe — Since 2003, Metacafe has been one of the world's top online video sites, currently attracting 25 million unique views per month. Displays new, emerging talents and Hollywood heavyweights alike.

Revver — An online media network with broad syndication reach and unique technology that pairs videos with targeted ads and tracks them as they spread virally across the Web so that "*no matter where your video travels, you benefit because we share the advertising revenue with you.*"

Vimeo — Cited by *PC World* as one of the 100 best products of 2008, this site even includes helpful hints on the creation of video content should you find yourself stuck in creative neutral.

VuMe — Another site that shares revenue with content providers. What's playing on VuMe? *"Everything from the serious to the humorous and the slick to the silly. If you can create it, it has a home on Vume."*

Another way to educate yourself about the world of web series is to check out the work of those considered to be the best in the field by their peers. Here is a list of nominees for the 2010 Streamy Awards, which bills itself as "the first and most prestigious awards ceremony devoted to honoring excellence in original web television programming and those who create it."

Best Comedy Web Series
Between Two Ferns with Zach Galifianakis
Easy to Assemble
The Guild
The Legend of Neil
Wainy Days

Best Drama Web Series
Angel of Death
Compulsions
OzGirl
The Bannen Way
Valemont

Best Foreign Web Series
Flying Kebab
Girl Number 9
Noob
OzGirl
Riese

Best New Web Series
$5 Cover: Memphis

Girl Number 9
Odd Jobs
Old Friends
The Bannen Way

Best Companion Web Series
Assassin's Creed: Lineage
Dexter: Early Cuts
Harper's Globe
The Office: Subtle Sexuality
Weeds: University of Andy

Best Animated Web Series
Eli's Dirty Jokes
Happy Tree Friends
Homestar Runner
How It Should Have Ended
Zero Punctuation

Best Branded Entertainment Web Series
Back on Topps (Topps)
Brainstorm (Altoids)
Easy to Assemble (IKEA)
Parts Art (Lexus)
The Temp Life (Spherion)

Best Experimental Web Series
Auto-Tune the News
Green Porno
HBO Cube
INST MSGS
Level 26

Best Directing for a Comedy Web Series
Blue Movies (Scott Brown)
Dorm Life: Semester 2 (Chris Smith, Mark Stewart Iverson)
James Gunn's PG Porn (James Gunn)
The Guild (Sean Becker)
The Legend of Neil (Sandeep Parikh)

Best Directing for a Drama Web Series
Anyone But Me (Tina Cesa Ward)
Compulsions (Nathan Atkinson)
Girl Number 9 (James Moran, Dan Turner)
The Bannen Way (Jesse Warren)
Young American Bodies (Joe Swanberg)

Best Writing for a Comedy Web Series
Back on Topps (Jason Sklar, Randy Sklar, Eric Friedman, Matt Price)
Dorm Life (Chris Smith, Jordan Riggs, Jessie Gaskell, Jack De Sena, Jim Brandon, Brian Singleton, Mark Stewart Iverson)
The Legend of Neil (Tony Janning, Sandeep Parikh)
The Guild (Felicia Day)
Wainy Days (David Wain)

Best Writing for a Drama Web Series
Anyone But Me (Susan Miller, Tina Cesa Ward)
Compulsions (Bernie Su)
Girl Number 9 (James Moran)
The Bannen Way (Jesse Warren, Mark Gantt)
Valemont (Christian Taylor)

Best Editing in a Web Series
$5 Cover: Memphis (Nathan Black, Morgan Jon Fox, Josh Swain)
Angel of Death (Jochen Kunstler, Jacob Vaughan)
Auto-Tune the News (Evan Gregory, Andrew Gregory, Michael Gregory)
I Kissed a Vampire (David Bekoff)
The Bannen Way (Zack Arnold)

Best Cinematography in a Web Series
Angel of Death (Carl Herse)
Circle of Eight (Michael Lohmann)
LUMINA (XiaoSu Han, Andreas Thalhammer)
Mountain Man (Robert Lam)
Riese (Christopher Charles Kempinski)

Best Art Direction in a Web Series
$99 Music Videos (Jack Ferry)

Green Porno (Rick Gilbert)
Mountain Man (Matt Enlow)
Riese (Chad Krowchuk)
Tiki Bar TV (Kim Bailey)

Best Sound Design in a Web Series
Fear Clinic (Kunal Rajan)
Mountain Man (Michael Miller)
Riese (Bill Mellow, Kevin Belen)
Rockville, CA (Seth Talley)
The Vetala (Randy Kiss)

And for the latest, up-to-the-minute information on current web series, be sure to check out my website at *www.bytesized.tv*.

Why Create For The Internet?

The reasons to create series for the Internet, as opposed to creating for other film or video outlets, are nearly as varied as the Internet itself. But the reasons are all linked, in a sense, by one word: **opportunity**.

First and foremost, the Internet offers **creative opportunity**. Broadcast and cable television are limited by all sorts of factors. They must, by necessity, appeal to a broad audience. Even if you could get a meeting with the head of a major broadcast network like CBS, she wouldn't consider buying your idea unless she thought it would appeal to at least ten million people, most of whom already watch CBS. The mandate to appeal to the widest possible audience is often why so much of network television is bland or derivative. Cable has more freedom, but is still restricted by tastes of their core audience, the channel's branding choices, potential advertiser objections, government regulations, and on and on. The Internet, on the other hand, allows you to create the kind of content *you* would want to watch and to seek out an audience with similar taste. Where two million regular viewers would be considered a flop on a broadcast network, it would be a phenomenon on the Internet. Take, for example, the acclaimed

Internet series *quarterlife*. The groundbreaking series attracted a loyal audience on the Net, not to mention financial support from major advertisers like Toyota and Pepsi. But NBC gave the broadcast version of the series exactly one airing before yanking it and unceremoniously tossing it on the network TV reject pile.

The Internet also offers **financial opportunity**. Hosting sites like Revver and VuMe match advertisers with content and share the revenue stream with creators. While it is highly unlikely you'll get rich this way, it is entirely possible to take in enough ad money to pay for the ongoing production of your series. Moreover, videomakers are invited to post their work at no charge, as opposed to most film and video festivals that charge an entry fee.

Another huge plus for webisodes is that they provide **career opportunity**. There are many students in universities, community colleges, high schools and even junior high schools who are bursting with creative ideas and video talent. They are ready, willing and able to make films today. But rare is the film studio or traditional media business willing to take a chance on "unproven" talent. The aspiring filmmaker, even one with a degree from a prestigious brand-name film school, usually finds he must start at the bottom, fetching coffee and running errands. It can easily be ten years or more before you've "paid your dues" and earned the opportunity to do what you set out to do in the first place — make films. On the Internet, however, all that matters is your work. You create your series, make your webisodes, post them, and let the audience decide if you're ready to direct or not.

Career opportunities also abound for working film and video professionals who want to stretch their creative boundaries. Maybe you're an assistant director, grip, gaffer, editor, or other worker in the film or television business who yearns to tell stories of his own but who will never be taken seriously as a potential writer/director because the industry has pigeonholed you as "crew" rather than "creative." The Internet makes it possible for you to sidestep the narrow-minded gatekeepers of Hollywood by investing your time and energy in making your own film rather than toiling thanklessly on someone else's vision.

Creative people in a variety of artistic pursuits are discovering the enormous power of the Internet to provide what might be called **exposure opportunity**. The Groundlings, a legendary Los Angeles improvisational theater troupe that has helped launch the careers of Lisa Kudrow, Will Ferrell, Phil Hartman and many others, has spent decades performing in their 99-seat theater. But after shooting the spoof *David Blaine Street Magic* in the alley behind their theater and posting it on YouTube, the video racked up 18 million plays. That's the power of the Internet. If the Groundlings performed the sketch in their theater to sold-out audiences every night, it would take 181,818 performances — more than 6,000 years — to reach an audience of 18 million. On the Internet, it happened in a matter of months and scored the group a contract to provide 50 webisodes for Crackle.

On the Internet, with dozens of hosting sites open to all, there are no gatekeepers to tell you why you can't do what you know you can, and virtually no limits to the size of the audience you can reach if your work goes viral and becomes a phenomenon. If you make a great web series (and you market it well — see Chapter Thirteen), the audience will find it. To paraphrase the mysterious voice in the cornfield in the film *Field of Dreams* — "If you build it, they will come."

In short, the Internet provides unlimited opportunity for anyone with the desire to create video content. In fact, the hunger for content is so voracious that the Internet is not just opening the doors of opportunity, it's begging you to come in and make yourself at home. But you need a bit more than desire and an idea. You need the fortitude to follow through on that idea. And you need the craft and skills to turn that vague idea into a high-quality polished pilot ready for digital distribution across the World Wide Web. Many have inspiration, but few have craft and know-how. That's what the following chapters are about: helping you to acquire those tools.

Are you ready? Good. Let's begin.

● FOR TEACHERS...

If you taught creative writing, you'd surely insist that your students study the techniques of the masters as a foundation for their own creative work. Music, art and film instructors also require their students to study outstanding works in the field, past and present. Short video is no different. Those who seek to be top creators should begin by studying the best work already done in the form. As an assignment in conjunction with Chapter One of this book, ask your students to watch three episodes of a current web series and write a short (two to three pages) paper analyzing the series.

For this analysis to be of depth and value, the student should not just casually surf the Net and stare blankly at a few videos, but must think and write critically about the work they view. At Goddard College, where I obtained my MFA in Creative Writing, we were required to write weekly "annotations," two- to three-page analyses of works of fiction, narrowly focused on a specific, noteworthy area of craft such how the main character was introduced, or image motifs, or use of location as a character. The idea was to train us, as readers, to examine in detail the underlying techniques used by the writer in constructing the work.

For short-form Internet series, students could focus on aspects of craft such as creating compelling main characters, or economy of storytelling, or techniques employed to maximize audience engagement. The students could also be asked to parse basic elements such as number of series characters, genre, production value (low, average or high), length of episodes, etc.

This assignment should be given not just during Week One, but regularly throughout the semester. Students of music and literature study other musicians as a regular part of their ongoing training. Aspiring webisode artists should be equally committed to the study of their form.

CHAPTER TWO
THE SERIES CONCEPT

In early 2007, when I first began teaching courses on making short-form TV series for the Internet, I was hard-pressed to find even a handful of examples to screen for my students. The early prototypes like *lonelygirl15* and *Sam Has 7 Friends* were around, but not much else. Now, at last count, there are approximately 187 gazillion web series to choose from — roughly one web series for every 18- to 30-year-old in the world currently cruising a bar looking for Mr. or Miss Right, or at least Mr. or Miss Right Now. Unfortunately, despite the abundance of web series and barflies, precious few are worth your time. In most cases, you can tell within seconds that your best move is to move on.

In the case of web series, there are basically two reasons why so many are so bad. Reason One: flawed concept. Reason Two: flawed execution. This chapter aims to prevent you from falling into the pit of despair and failure that inevitably waits; no matter how slick your execution is, if you start out with a flawed concept.

What makes for a good web series premise? While there is no formula for success, it makes sense to study what's been done and take note of what has worked and what has flopped. As Mark Twain once said, "History doesn't repeat itself, but it rhymes." So let's start by taking a look at some really bad rhymes and try not to repeat them.

Fatally Flawed Series Concepts

I once asked a former ABC comedy development executive, who spent five years hearing thousands of concept pitches from writers, what the single worst idea for a series was that a writer ever brought in. She cocked her head, gave it a few seconds of serious consideration — perhaps trying to debate between hundreds of equally bad ideas — then nodded confidently and said, "Talking drapes." I responded the only way I could: *Talking drapes? What the fu...?* She said absolutely, a writer — not a newbie, or one who had lost his mind, all evidence to the contrary, but a writer with a solid resume filled with major TV and feature film credits — came in and pitched a series about a man who buys a spooky fixer-upper of a house and soon discovers that the drapes are inhabited by a wise-cracking spirit that speaks to him in one-liners.

Like most writers, I relish all opportunities to mock the competition, so I repeated the talking drapes story to a friend who actually knew the writer who had pitched it. My friend called the writer and said, "You actually pitched a series to ABC about talking drapes?" The talking drapes writer, without hesitation, shot back indignantly, "Look, that could have worked."

When it comes to creativity and art, there's no predicting what can or will work. And sometimes even the most unlikely notion, in the hands of gifted writers, directors and performers, becomes successful, possibly even critically acclaimed. (Think *Seinfeld*, a show that proudly proclaims to be about "nothing.") But some ideas are just so wrong that they deserve to be thrown under the bus like disgraced politicians.

The most common mistake in formulating a pitch for a web series is thinking something is a series when it's really just a one-shot (or three-shot, at best) idea. As the word *series* implies, your idea must contain characters and a premise that can be mined for subsequent episodes over and over again. So if you attempt to make a series called *Zippy and Skippy*, about the hilarious things that occur when you smear peanut butter on your Golden Retriever Zippy's genitals and he tries to lick it off, you may end up with a humorous 60 seconds of video (though the folks at PETA will be steamed) but you won't have shot a series pilot. Why not? Because there's no Episode 2. You've exhausted all the stories that the Skippy on Zippy premise can sustain. And no, smearing chunky instead of creamy, or switching to cream cheese on the cat's privates wouldn't count as different stories any more than changing from Little Red to Little Blue Riding Hood would.

A good series concept must have "legs" — that is, the ability to be used for lots and lots of episodic stories based on that premise, regardless of whether the episodes are 60 minutes or 60 seconds in length. The one exception to this rule is if you are doing, in essence, a soap opera or serialized version of a long story. In that case, your series will consist of one long, extended story that is broken up into chapters — each chapter being an episode. But if you go the serialized route, you should probably take a few minutes and jot down what you think the first dozen or so installments might cover, rather than just writing a pilot and then discovering your story runs out of gas after Episode 3.

To illustrate the difference between a concept with legs and one without, let me once again cite an example from half-hour network television that most people will be familiar with: *Seinfeld*. The central premise of *Seinfeld* (despite its claim to be about "nothing") is that of four neurotic, dysfunctional friends in New York City and the neurotic, dysfunctional adventures they get into dealing with the everyday minutia of life. Clearly there are dozens of episodes or "installments" that can be written based on Jerry, Elaine, Kramer and George and this basic premise. NBC aired 180 of them over the show's nine-year run, and they continue to rerun in syndication worldwide.

But let's say, for the sake of illustration, that instead of focusing on Jerry and the gang, you decide that one of the random characters they meet on their adventures — let's say The Soup Nazi — is the funniest character in all of New York City, and therefore should be the center of your show. Big mistake. As funny as The Soup Nazi was in one episode, his character and premise — how his dictatorial management style terrorizes customers — does not provide a good central premise for a series. Why not? Because there is basically only one story or episode that would be repeated over and over — the customer comes in, The Soup Nazi cops an attitude and shouts, "You, no soup, two weeks!" There won't be stories for Episodes 2, 3, 4 or 44. All you can do is write Episode 1, 1A, 1B, 1C, *ad infinitum*. And nobody will stick around for any of the subsequent episodes because after watching your pilot, their reaction to any of the others will be *I've already seen this.*

Another common mistake in choosing a premise is making it so personal and obscure that the only audience that can possibly be in on the joke is... well, *you*. Even though one of the oldest adages about writing is *write what you know*, if what you know is impossible for anyone else to understand or relate to, then what you write may have a potential audience of exactly one.

Let's say you work at a plumbing supply store. Better yet, let's say you work as a regional sales rep for a wholesale plumbing supply distributor that sells to the major hardware and home improvement stores in the Mid-Atlantic states. You've done this for 20 years, had a ton of laughs along the way with all the weird characters who've been your customers, and feel certain there's a great Internet comedy with hundreds of hilarious episodes based on your daily work life. Even has a great title: *Flushed!* Practically writes itself.

Unfortunately, *Flushed!* will probably go right down the drain, because to understand most of the humor you and your fellow plumbing parts pals have shared, you need to be in the plumbing supply business, or at least be familiar with the names of all the major parts of a toilet. As hilarious as you think it is when Ernie from Ernie's Hardware of Baltimore says, "Whatever floats your float rod," or when Del from Home Depot of Dover, Delaware, responds to your question about restocking his ballcock supply with a pithy, "That's what she said," you, Ernie and

Del may be the only ones laughing. Your series premise doesn't have to appeal to everyone. But the comedy or drama must be accessible beyond your immediate circle of friends and coworkers if you hope to attract an audience of any significant size.

Be Bold, Fresh And Original

The above warning not withstanding, you must also avoid the opposite temptation — namely to be so "universal" in appeal that all you are doing is recycling pale imitations of old concepts that have already been successful. Today's Internet video consumer has literally millions of options to choose from. If you want to grab his attention, you must begin with a concept that makes him say *Oooh, that sounds interesting.* Clones and knock-offs don't do that. "It's like *Cheers,* but instead of a bar, it's set in a Laundromat" won't make anyone grab anything but their head.

So what has worked? Let's take a look at a few successful Internet series and analyze what made each premise attractive. To make sure we're focusing on premise rather than other factors, we'll exclude series made by known Hollywood players like Ed Zwick and Marshall Herskovitz (*quarterlife*) or that include recognizable on-camera talent, like *Dr. Horrible's Sing-Along Blog* starring Neil Patrick Harris. Those types of series, due to their star power either in front of or behind the camera, get press coverage to help them promote the show and draw an initial supply of viewers. Most of you won't have access to that sort of publicity machine and will, therefore, have to come up with a concept that makes the video surfers of the world say *I've gotta check that out.*

The Guild

Before Felicia Day became an Internet Goddess, she was a working actress. Barely. She'd had some modest success, including a recurring part as "Vi" in the final season of the cult TV series *Buffy The Vampire Slayer.* But she grew tired of waiting for the phone to ring, hoping some unknown producer or director would deign to offer her a part, so she took matters into her own hands and created a TV series for herself. A longtime video game addict (she's a Level 66 gnome warlock and a Level 63 priest in *World of Warcraft* according to *geeksaresexy.net*), Day decided to write what she knew best and created *The Guild* (*watchtheguild.com*), a comedy web series about online gamers and their relationships with each other both online and off. In the pilot episode, Day's character "Codex" (her online gamer name) is fired by her therapist for refusing to admit she has an addiction to video games. Things get even worse for Codex when fellow gamer Zaboo shows up at her apartment, convinced that because Codex "winkied" him online, she's hot for his bod and they're destined to be an item.

What makes this a good web series premise? First and foremost, it appeals to an audience that spends a huge amount of time online, namely online video gamers. While humor about plumbing supplies and toilet parts would be met with a blank stare by the cyber-geek crowd, this group totally gets what a "winkie" is. And they totally get how addicted you can get to video games, and how your fellow addicts become your friends and perhaps more, whether you like it or not.

Day originally wrote *The Guild* as a half-hour pilot but was told the subject matter was "too niche" for network or cable TV. Probably true. But it's perfect for the web series world because that's where the natural audience for a series about online gamers is — online.

Day partnered with Kim Evey, who had coproduced the successful web series *Tiny Gorgeous Chicken Machine Show* (on Crackle). Day and Evey self-financed the first three episodes of *The Guild*. The episodes were successful in that they attracted a loyal and sizeable audience, but Day and Evey ran out of enough money to continue the show. Then they got a brilliant idea. Why not see if the fans of the show would pay for more episodes? They put a Paypal button up on the existing episodes, solicited contributions, and — lo and behold — the viewers sent in the money. Not "get rich quick and retire to Tahiti" money, mind you. But enough money to finance production for the rest of Season 1.

There can be no better proof that you are doing something right than to have an audience who has been receiving something for free voluntarily send you money so you can keep doing it. And in the end, both the audience and Day were rewarded further. *The Guild*'s grassroots success became a story, one that caught the attention of Microsoft, who agreed to sponsor the show for Season 2 (and later more) and to put it on its newly launched Xbox Independent Video Channel online.

The bottom line is this: know your potential audience. If your audience is online, then your premise should appeal to some group of people who spend a fair amount of time online. They don't have to be gamers or Facebook addicts or other online junkies necessarily, but the show you create should appeal in tone, subject matter, style or some other way to those who spend a significant amount of time online.

Gaytown and *General Elevator*

Gaytown (on Crackle) is about a closeted heterosexual man in a predominantly gay world trying to do straight guy things without being "outed." Our hero yearns to play basketball (with the girls) because all the "normal" boys just do ballet and will beat the living snot out of you with their designer shoes if they find out you're a hetero "pervert." In the pilot our straight hero gets busted by undercover gay cops for secretly meeting other heteros in a public toilet to play fantasy football.

General Elevator (originally on National Banana and now on YouTube) is a soap opera spoof that takes place entirely in the elevator of a hospital. It parodies the potboiler plotlines and extreme melodrama of daytime serials like *General Hospital* and includes a token black doctor named Dr. Oreo, pronounced o-RAY-o.

The concepts couldn't be more different. So why have I grouped them together? Because they share one essential quality in common — you can explain the premise and give people a sense of where the humor will come from in only a few words. Making the premise easy to understand — and easy to explain — is essential for a short-form series. If each episode is to run about five minutes, it better not take four minutes just to explain the basic idea. The online entertainment audience has a notoriously short attention span. If you want to grab their attention, you must do it quickly. Even if the execution of your series will have subtleties, complexities and nuances, make sure the basic concept can be conveyed simply, quickly and clearly. With *Gaytown* and *General Elevator*, the titles themselves come close to explaining each show's premise.

Some other examples of simple, clear premises:

Black Version

(from 60Frames now on YouTube)

African-American parodies of famous movie scenes; e.g., the "Black Version" of the fake orgasm scene in *When Harry Met Sally*, wherein the woman's passionate talk during her simulated orgasm is ridiculously over the top (including cuts where she's suddenly wearing a blond wig), and yet the man still believes it was real and walks away even more cocky about his sexual prowess.

The Ed Hardy Boyz

(on Funny Or Die)

A twist on the squeaky-clean Hardy Boys series, where instead the "detectives" are two *dese, dem* and *dose* Jersey goofballs who wear Ed Hardy clothing and try to solve mysteries while hitting on any available woman with lines like, "Excuse me, do youse two play for an Anaheim baseball team? Because you're both angels."

What The Buck

(on YouTube)

Imagine if Jack from *Will & Grace* had his own online celebrity dish program. Michael Buckley took $6 worth of fabric for a backdrop, a pair of work lights from Home Depot, a video camera, and his catty approach to celebrity dish and turned it into 2008's most popular entertainment program on YouTube, with more than 100 million views.

Hot For Words

(on YouTube or *hotforwords.com*)

Okay, here's the premise: an Eastern European philologist explains the etymology (linguistic history) of words such as *scrumtrilescent* and *pulchritudinous*. Sounds like a complete snooze, you say? Perhaps I left out one crucial detail. Here is your *Hot For Words* host and instructor:

Photo by Justin Price

Has your passion for philology and etymology just taken a gigantic leap? No, it's not porn, but Marina Orlova, who holds degrees in Teaching of Russian Language and World Literature and Teaching of English Language Specializing in Philology, and definitely has the kind of classroom presence that holds students' attention — at least male students who aren't residents of Gaytown. She launched *Hot For Words* on YouTube in mid-2007 and within a year racked up more than 150 million views. Her success caught the attention of cable TV news mogul Bill O'Reilly, who booked her for multiple guest appearances and tutorials, and she was voted 5th sexiest woman on the Web by

G4 TV (which begs the question *This woman's only number five? Yikes — just who the heck are numbers one through four?!*)

A picture is worth a thousand words, and when you check out Marina Orlova's site, you get to learn the thousand words as well. Those of you hoping to learn a new word a day will be thrilled to learn that Marina has a wall calendar.

The point is Marina Orlova really does have a passion for language and words. But she found a way to package that passion to capture an audience. Her premise is simple to understand, easy to sell visually (online video is, after all, visual), and has the entire unabridged dictionary as a source for potential future episodes.

And by the way, *pulchritudinous*, as Ms. Orlova explains in coy detail, means beautiful, sexy, hot, gorgeous, alluring — she goes on for a while with the synonyms, each one delivered with the subtext *you want me and you know it*. How in the world did Marina ever find the word pulchritudinous, I wonder?

So Where's The Drama?

Good question. While there is no law saying that all Internet TV series must be comedies or reality series, the vast majority fall into one of those two categories. The reason, I suspect, is that drama is a much trickier proposition when the average length of an episode is only three to five minutes. It's difficult to build the elements crucial to drama, like suspense, tension, character arc and so on, in that restricted amount of time. In theory, you can just take a longer drama, like a one-hour network series or a feature film, and break it into smaller parts. But the reality is, it's a huge challenge to re-establish dramatic elements and the heightened emotions that drama demands each and every episode. It would be a bit like having to stop your car every block or two, turn off the engine, then pop the hood and break out the jumper cables to get it going again. The journey takes more effort than it's worth.

That said, there are some successful short-form dramas on the Internet, like *quarterlife*. (There have also been some noteworthy examples of high-budget dramas like *Sanctuary* and *The Bannen*

Way, which were made for the Web but were also designed — if the episodes were edited together consecutively — as feature films.) If drama is your thing, or you have a premise for a drama in mind that you think can really work on the Internet, have at it. But be aware of the challenges of sustaining audience involvement. One way *quarterlife* addressed this issue was to shoot several episodes before posting any. The audience could watch in small bites if they wanted, but they could also click through and watch more episodes if they got hooked on the pilot, instead of having to wait another month for Episode 2, then another month for Episode 3, and so on.

You Need A Killer Title

Though technically not part of the premise of your series, coming up with a killer title is just as important to the success of your web series as devising a solid premise. Your title is the first thing that gets a potential viewer to either click through and view or click away and move on. Your goal is a title that both *tells* and *sells* — in other words, a title that both clearly communicates what your series is about (tells) and makes the audience say *yes I want to see that* (sells). Remember: the Internet video revolution means potential viewers have literally millions of video entertainment products to choose from. Your title has to not just grab their attention, but make web video surfers stop, click, and watch.

For my money, here are some strong titles that tell me what the show will be about before I even see it and make me want to sample an episode or two:

Gaytown
We Need Girlfriends
Web Therapy

Each of these titles gives me a pretty good idea of what the show is about and hints at the type of humor the show might have — the hook that gets me to watch. A title can also be effective if it's not exactly clear, but is so "out there" or bizarre that it makes people want to click through just to see what the heck it is. *Gorgeous Tiny Chicken Machine Show*, while it turned out to be a series I didn't personally care for, was certainly a compelling enough title that I had to see what it was all about. *The Ninety-Year-Old Hooker*, on the other hand, is a title (of a non-existent show) that, while perfectly clear, may not be the right bait to lure predominantly young Internet video audiences.

● FOR TEACHERS...

Students can benefit from two types of premise assignments — analytical and creative. The analytical work can provide context and illumination in preparation for the students' own creative work.

For the analytical assignment, they can write a short analysis of two or three web series and why their premise is effective, or why it isn't. As in the previous chapter, the key to success in this assignment is specificity. A simple thumbs up or thumbs down is useless. What is of value is developing the students' ability to critically examine the inner architecture of the video series they see on the Web.

For the creative, they can pitch a premise for an original web series that they will write a pilot script for later in the semester. I usually ask my students to come in with two series ideas — one fully developed, the other less so. "Fully developed" means they can explain the premise, define the main series characters, and give a sense of the tone, style and type of stories the series will present.

I require my students to write the idea down on paper, but to also be prepared to pitch it verbally. The verbal pitch is the standard methodology of television and film, and so even shy writers must learn a bit of salesmanship and verbal presentation skills if they are to succeed in this world. But requiring them to put their pitch on paper as well forces them to examine it more closely than if they just "wing it" with a verbal pitch — one they might cook up about three minutes before class if they aren't required to put something on paper as well.

CHAPTER THREE
CREATING COMPELLING CHARACTERS

While your title may be the bait that lures viewers into sampling your series, your characters are the primary ingredient that keeps them coming back for meal after meal. Quick: name some of the most memorable network TV series of all time. Here's my "off the top of my head" list:

I Love Lucy
The Mary Tyler Moore Show
All In The Family
Happy Days
The Simpsons
Law & Order

The first two have the main character's name right in the title of the show. Why? Because that character (and performer) is the main reason people watched the series week after week. In fact, people most often referred to these two landmark series simply by the character's name, as in *Did you see the Lucy where she works in the chocolate factory?*

What about the next two? No names in those titles. Still, what's the first thing that comes to mind when I say *All In The Family*? Archie Bunker, of course. Yes, the series had brilliant writing and embraced ground-breaking, provocative subject matter like impotence, menopause and racism. But it was the phenomenal popularity of Archie Bunker (and Edith, the Meathead, and Archie's "little girl" Gloria) that was the primary driver of the series' breakout and long-lasting popularity.

Same goes for *Happy Days*, the nostalgic half-hour comedy about suburban middle-class life in the 1950s. Ask anyone to say the first thing that comes to mind when you mention the show *Happy Days*, I'd lay odds that 95 out of 100 people would instantly say "The Fonz" — and then 80 of those 95 would pretend to comb back their "DA" hairstyle and say "Ayyyyy!" just like The Fonz. Ironically, the character of Arthur "The Fonz" Fonzarelli wasn't supposed to be the star of *Happy Days*. In the pilot, he was a minor character who had half a dozen lines. But the audience loved The Fonz, as played by Henry Winkler, and that love launched *Happy Days* to the top of the ratings heap. How powerful a character was The Fonz? In the months after the show aired an episode where he got a library card for the first time, more than a million kids nationwide went to their local library and signed up for their first library card — so they could be just like The Fonz. That's a powerful character.

It's no accident that CBS and ABC paid Carroll O'Connor and Henry Winkler record sums to continue playing Archie and The Fonz year after year. The networks knew that without those characters (and the actors playing those characters) the audience would tune out.

Even with shows like *The Simpsons* and *Law & Order*, ensembles with many characters and either brilliant humor or riveting storylines, the characters drive the popularity and long-term audience appeal of the shows. People love *The Simpsons* because of the great characters, both the main ones like Bart and Homer, and the peripheral ones like Apu or Krusty the Klown. And as for the *Law & Order* franchise, I suspect the audience chooses which particular *L&O* series to watch (*Special Victims, Criminal Intent*, or the original) based on which set of characters they like rather than what sort of crimes are dealt with.

The importance of character cannot be overstated. There have been zillions of medical shows, cop shows and family sitcoms on television over the years. But the shows that succeeded — and which continue to bring audiences back to watch them even fifty years later in reruns worldwide — are the ones where the characters made a powerful and lasting impression on the audience. You might say that it's just a function of the actor and his or her popularity, but you would be wrong. Bill Cosby has had several TV series, but only when he played Dr. Heathcliff Huxtable, beleaguered but affable father of five, did he achieve megastar status. Same thing for Mary Tyler Moore. Even today, more than thirty years past the series' final installment, most people remember her fondly as Mary Richards. But almost no one remembers her, fondly or otherwise, as Annie McGuire (the title character of her 1988 ABC series that disappeared faster than the fifth runner-up on *American Idol*).

Yes, you need great actors — and we'll talk quite a bit about how to find them in Chapter Nine. But actors need great characters in order to do great work. And audiences need great characters in order to return to a series episode after episode. Here's Blake Snyder, in his screenwriting book *Save The Cat!*, explaining the overriding importance of character, or who your story is about:

> The "who" is our way in. We, the audience, zero in on and project onto the "who" whether it's an epic motion picture or a commercial for Tide detergent. The "who" gives us someone to identify with... because it's easier to communicate an idea when someone is standing there experiencing it for us. And whether we're watching *Lawrence of Arabia* as Lawrence tries to figure out how to attack Acaba... or a Tylenol commercial in which a busy Soccer Mom wonders when her headache will go away, the principle of involving us in the story is the same.

Characters, especially your main character, are what compel people to come back to your little video party week after week. Think of your main character as the host of your party — or, more accurately, your series of parties. He greets the guests at the door, sets the tone for the experience. The audience decision about whether to return for the next installment of your particular party is based largely on how they feel about the host. Is he someone they want to hang out with again and again? Or is he a tiresome bore who makes them say *screw the free guacamole, we're outta here!*

Character Essentials

Okay, you get it. You need to have great characters. But what makes for a great character? Broad strokes? Fine details? Larger than life traits? Probably all of the above. But I think a good place to start is by saying that all truly great characters have to **resonate** with us. That is, they must strike us as real — not ordinary or trite, but familiar in a way that makes us say *that's just like my boss* or *I knew a guy in high school just like that.*

For all of Archie Bunker's flaws, he rings true to us. We've all got a blowhard uncle like Archie. Or a neighbor. Or maybe even a small, less than appealing part of ourselves. Norman Lear, who developed *All In The Family* for American television (it was based on a British show called *Till Death Do Us Part*) once called Archie Bunker "basically a horse's ass." But Lear also remarked that Archie was "the bigger-than-life epitome of something that's in all of us, like it or not." In other words, the character resonates.

While web series, because of their much shorter episode length, cannot create characters in as much depth as a 30- or 60-minute network TV show, or a two-hour feature film, the principles of character are no less relevant. The characters in your short-form series, especially the main character, must resonate with the audience. Take *The Guild* as an example. Microsoft bought the show for its Xbox online channel because it knows the channel's natural audience — online game fanatics — will instantly relate to *The Guild's* characters — a bunch of online game fanatics. The audience *gets* the show's characters like Codex and Zaboo. They know their world, understand their video-obsessive behavior and gamer lingo. And because they know (and like) these people, they want to attend their party — the episodes of *The Guild* — time after time.

Does this mean the only people who can enjoy *The Guild* are online gaming addicts? Absolutely not, any more than the only people who enjoy *All In The Family* are bigots and fools. For a character to resonate, or be relatable, he doesn't have to be "just like you." He only has to be recognizable — meaning he might be like you, or might be like someone you know or have somehow encountered in your life.

The next essential element of all great series characters is that **we can instantly imagine those characters in dozens of juicy situations** — juicy in either a comedic or dramatic way, depending on the tone of the series. Let's return to The Soup Nazi from *Seinfeld* once again. Great character for an episode or two — fabulous "guest star" or peripheral character. Terrific spice, but not a good main ingredient. Because as hilarious and memorable as The Soup Nazi was for that classic episode, he's not a good choice for a regular series character and definitely NOT the lead character you can base an entire series around. Where do you take The Soup Nazi other than his restaurant to get stories? What other situations can you put him in? I suppose you could send him on a date, or meet his family — maybe there's a Soup Nazi Sr. or Grandma Soup Nazi, and we see not only where The Soup Nazi came from but gain a measure of sympathy for him as an improved version of his predecessors. But when you boil it down, every episode becomes nothing more than repetition after repetition of the same basic gag: "You, no second date, two months!"

For a series regular, a character you see in each and every episode of a series, to be truly useful that character must have depth and dimension. In other words, he or she must be a human character, not a two-dimensional caricature. If Archie Bunker had merely been a malaprop-spouting bigot, *All In The Family* would never have lasted as long as it did. It would have been a one-joke pony. But Archie was a dimensional human being, a man born and raised in one time railing against the rapidly changing world around him. A man stuck in one time fighting against change stimulates dozens of situations and ideas. A bigot? Not so many.

The third vital element of all good series characters is **specifics**. The devil is always in the details. If I say "car," you probably get a picture in your head, but it's blurry and out of focus until

I get more specific. For instance, if I say "sports car" or "SUV," the picture in your head is now sharper and a lot more specific. Better still would be "red Ferrari" or "black Hummer." Now we know precisely what we're talking about — and we have a much clearer sense of the "character" we're talking about than we did when we simply said "car."

Specifics are what make a character. If I ask you who your main character is, and you say "She's a waitress," you really haven't told me much, and certainly haven't sketched any details that make me want to watch a series about "a waitress." You need more specifics. Waitress at an elite eatery in New York City or a greasy spoon in Buttscratch, Oklahoma? Is she 22 or 52? Is this Madison Kemp's first day at TGIFriday's — a job she only plans to keep until she sells that novel (or Internet video series) she's been working on since high school? Or does today mark thirty years at the Buttscratch Eat-'n'-Gas for Nadine and the chef celebrates the occasion by putting a candle in a sausage patty and leading the regulars in a hearty chorus of "Happy Anniversary"? They're both waitresses, but Madison and Nadine are two entirely different characters — which means the stories you tell about them, and how they react and behave in the situations those stories present, will be vastly different. It's all about the details.

In *The Guild*, all the characters are online gaming freaks. But aside from that shared video addiction, they are all distinct individuals. Here is the character breakdown for *The Guild* from its Wikipedia page:

- **Codex** — Real name: Cyd Sherman. She is the healer (Priest). Codex was a child prodigy violinist, but now she is older and is at a crossroads in her life. Her father and ex-boyfriend are both gay and she has a tendency not to leave the house for weeks at a time. In the first episode she is trying to control the amount of time she spends online per day but ultimately fails, which leads to her therapist "breaking up" with her. Since Season 1, Zaboo has moved in with her, against her will, and followed her to her new house when she was forced to move. Codex is played by Felicia Day.

- **Zaboo** — Real name: Sujan Balakrishnan Goldberg. He is the Gnome Warlock of the guild. Shows up at Codex's house because he thinks they are dating. This turns out to be partially true because Codex has problems with the colon (:) and semicolon (;) when sending smiley faces and tends to type winks instead. Zaboo is a HinJew, a combination of Hindu and Jew. He likes to work with Photoshop and created a picture of Zaboo and Codex with her DMV photo. He also has a tendency to say words with "'d" on the end, such as "photoshopp'd" and "doorstepp'd". Played by Sandeep Parikh.

- **Bladezz** — Real name: Simon. Bladezz is the guild Rogue. Clara describes him as the guild's retarded cousin. He has a tendency to hit on all the female guild mates. He has a little sister and appears to be about high school or college age. To pay for college, Bladezz works secretly as a male model and was humiliated when his Guild-mates found out. Played by Vincent Caso.

- **Vork** — Real name: Herman Holden. He is the guild leader and fighter (Warrior). He enjoys managing the guild and budgeting. He took care of his grandfather full-time until the previous summer when he died. Vork still receives his grandfather's social security checks in the mail, which is how he supports himself. Played by Jeff Lewis.

- **Clara** — Real name: Clara. She is the guild's Gnome Mage. Clara is a stay-at-home mother of three. Her three children are all young, with the youngest still breastfeeding. Clara is a little scatterbrained and an irresponsible mother, doing things like leaving her children in the car while at the guild meeting. Played by Robin Thorsen.

- **Tinkerballa** — Real name: Tinkerballa (as far as the guild knows). She is the guild's ranger (Hunter). Tink is another young member of the guild, high school or college aged. She distances herself from the guild trying not to let them know anything about her personal life. When asked what she does for a living she gives the plot to *Ugly Betty*. She is known for her sweet face, and not so sweet mouth, along with her almost constant need to be entertained by video games, playing a Nintendo DS while raiding and at the meeting. Played by Amy Okuda.

- **Wade** — First appearing in Season 2, Wade is Codex's hot neighbor. Not a gamer himself, Wade works as a martial arts stunt double, who comes into contact with Codex after she accidentally pushes him down some stairs. He's fond of showing off his moves and flirting with Codex, making her extremely nervous. Wade is played by Fernando Chien.

When you create your characters, be as specific as you can. BUT — and this is absolutely crucial — you must also make sure that the specifics you lay out about your character are relevant, telling, that they reveal important things about who your character is on the inside. A laundry list of random details about someone is useless unless those details reveal something significant about who that character is, how she might behave or react to the world around her. Just saying your main character Susie's least favorite color is blue and she has a pet parrot are specifics — they're just not terribly revealing or important. They don't tell us much about Susie or the kind of person she is. If, however, Susie hates blue, the parrot is blue, and the parrot used to belong to her hypercritical mother who loved blue, and now the parrot mocks and criticizes Susie's every move just like mom used to do — *that's significant*.

Characterization

Character is something internal — the essence of who a person is. So how do you take this internal thing — a person's essence — and communicate that essence to your audience? Answer: through **characterization**.

Characterization simply means the techniques by which you communicate internal character to us. It is the externalization or dramatization of the internal. And great news, boys and girls — when you get right down to it, there are really only three ways for you to convey or reveal who the characters in your series are: what they say (**dialogue**), what they do (**action**), and the **environment** they create, like their clothes, car, job and living situation.

Forget about writing for the moment and think about real life. When you meet someone new, how do you decide who they are, what kind of person they are, etc.? By taking careful note of exactly the details stated above. Each of us is kind of like The Terminator, with an involuntary mental computer that constantly processes data about the world and people around us. You walk into a Starbucks, spot a woman at a nearby table. The computer kicks in: she's in her thirties dressed in designer casual clothes, texting on her Blackberry with one hand while alternately sipping a chai latte and sharing her oat bran muffin with a toddler in a stroller. Two cars are parked out front: a nearly new Toyota hybrid SUV and a mud-caked 40-year-old VW van with flowers painted on it. Which car is hers? You can make a pretty good guess because you already know — or think you know — her "character." You know who she is, how she thinks, and can probably predict what kind of car she'd buy.

You walk out of Starbucks and on the sidewalk out front is a guy in his early sixties, long graying hair and a beard, playing a beat up old guitar with a peace sign painted on it. He's singing songs like Bob Dylan's "Blowin' in the Wind" and Barry McGuire's "Eve of Destruction." Based on these clues, your mental computer says *hippie refugee from the 1960s*. Now you have a pretty good idea who owns the VW van. And you probably can make all kinds of other character assessments. Did he vote for McCain or Obama? Or maybe he didn't vote at all *because that's how The Man controls you, man, and we've all got to fight the power.*

In a sense, the process of creating your characters is an inversion of the process you use to figure out who people are in the real world. As a writer, you will first decide who you want your characters to be, then your task is finding the ways to communicate that "who" to your audience. Let's turn to the 60Frames web series *Be a Celebutante*. The main characters are two rich, spoiled, less than intelligent party sluts whose only interests are money, self-indulgence, and hooking up — and helping you learn how to live the same charmed and fulfilling lifestyle. The pilot — which runs all of 95 seconds — is chock-full of character clues. Two hotties in bathing suits and fur shawls lounge by a private pool (**environment**). They introduce themselves as "the Douche (pronounced "doo-shay") sisters, heiresses to the douche fortune" (**dialogue**). They are drinking and dispensing smug advice on how to make extra money (**action**). Dannah and Danielle's ideas include:

>   DANNAH
> If you really want to rake in the
> dough...
>
>   DANIELLE
> Or make money...
>
>   DANNAH
> You should "accidentally" make a sex
> tape.

CUT TO FOOTAGE OF THE DOUCHE SISTERS IN BED WITH A MAN, CLEARLY AWARE OF THE CREW AS THEY "ACCIDENTALLY" MAKE A SEX TAPE.

>   DANNAH
> Yeah, when our "accidental" sex
> tape "accidentally" leaked onto the
> Internet, we "accidentally" made five
> million dollars.
>
>   DANIELLE
> Oopsies!

You get the idea. Everything your characters say, do, wear, drive, eat or come in contact with should tell us something about who they are as a person. Once the audience picks up on who they are (and hopefully finds them amusing or interesting enough to follow around for six or twelve or a hundred episodes), the audience also begins to anticipate the juicy situations you might put them in.

Your Overall Character Landscape

Characters do not exist in a vacuum. They exist to serve the overall premise, and exist in concert with each other. It's not enough for each individual character to be cool or interesting in his own right. They must work together, as a team, with the whole being greater than the sum of the parts. Each character should serve a specific function within your series, and that function should be unique. You wouldn't want a rock band with five lead singers but no drummer or bass player. Instead of Hootie and the Blowfish you end up with Hootie, Hootie, Hootie, Hootie and Hootie. Even Hootie's mom wouldn't want to see that act. The premise is *band*. The characters must form a complete team or group, one with stars *and* supporting players.

I think of this overall character composition as the **character landscape**. Your series landscape needs balance and variety. Each character should cover a different "instrument," a distinct function or sound within your overall composition. Take *The Guild* once again. Yes, they are all online gaming freaks. But aside from that, they are different types of people — a mom so addicted to video games that she virtually ignores her three young children (Clara); a young woman so afraid of revealing any real details about her personal life that when asked what she does for a living, she gives the plotline to *Ugly Betty* (Tinkerballa); and even, starting in Season 2, Codex's hottie neighbor who has absolutely no interest in video games at all (Wade). Characters with distinct differences are crucial to the success of your series because character differences are what lead to **conflict** — the essence of all comedy and drama and, therefore, the life-giving reservoir of stories for your pilot and your series.

Leading Characters vs. Supporting Characters

All series have both. As stated before, no good group can be composed of all Hooties (leading character) or all Blowfish (supporting characters). But why is Hootie (or Mick Jagger or Bono) the leading character? What makes him more important? Surprisingly, the answer is pretty much the same for both music videos and series television. *Your lead character is the center of gravity for your group.*

In a music video, the camera focuses on the lead singer more than anyone else. And when the camera isn't on the main character, what we see is mostly seen through his eyes. In a television series, we experience most of the action through the lead character's eyes. In *Gaytown*, the lead character is the straight person who is desperately trying to avoid detection and persecution. We follow the action of *Gaytown* from his POV, as opposed to, say, the perspective of a morals cop trying to track down the "perverted heterosexuals." We experience the world of *The Guild* primarily through the eyes of Codex. In *Seinfeld*, Jerry is the lead character, the primary prism through which the story is filtered.

So what makes these characters leads as opposed to supporting players? What makes these characters capable of anchoring a series? For one, as quirky and troubled as Jerry and Codex are, they are, from most of the audience's perspective, the most "normal" person in the universe of the series. Yes, Jerry on *Seinfeld* is a neurotic mess. But compared to George or Elaine or Kramer, he's a rock. Same goes for Codex. She's so warped even her therapist abandons her. But compared to Zaboo or Tinkerballa, she's a solid citizen. So one job description of your leading or main character might be *the sanest person in an insane world*. (Note: the rock band analogy breaks down here. There is no rule that says the lead singer of a rock band must be the sanest or most normal. He is free to have as many substance abuse and legal problems as he chooses. In fact, in the world of rock and roll, the more messed up you are, the higher your profile.)

Drawing On Real Life

So where do characters come from? Do they just pop into your imagination randomly? Of course not. Creative **inspiration**, despite the mystery that often surrounds that concept, is usually quite methodical. Inspiration comes because you work at it. William Faulkner once said, "I only write when I feel like it. Fortunately, I feel like it every day at 9 a.m."

Your characters will come to you because you work at it — conscientiously, purposefully, by design. To begin with, you've got your premise. Let's say it's *Seinfeld*, where the premise is, more or less: a stand-up comic observes and comments on the small insanities of life, and he lives in the capital of insanity, New York City. That's the roots of the world that series creators Jerry Seinfeld and Larry David began with. So their task, then, in developing that premise was to figure out *who do we surround Jerry with*? Rather than randomly spitballing a few zany characters off the top of their heads, Seinfeld and David did something incredibly logical: they were writing about the world they knew, so they chose real-life characters they knew (or fictitious versions of them) to be the supporting players. Believe it or not, Kramer is actually based on a real person that Larry David knew in New York — Kenny Kramer. (If you are so inclined, you can visit the real Kramer's website, *kennykramer.com*, and take his personal tour of New York City.) George is more or less based on Larry David himself. Not each and every detail — George isn't a writer. But emotionally, and in the neurotic way his mind functions (in other words, his "essence or character"), George is based on Larry David.

Real life is always the richest resource for fiction. Not a stereotyped version of real life, but keenly observed, specific details of real-life people. When Felicia Day developed the character landscape for *The Guild*, she didn't have to just imagine a bunch of characters. She could draw on the types of people she knew among her *World of Warcraft* playing friends and other online gaming acquaintances.

Drawing on real life is what allows you to be specific rather than generic. Let's say you wanted to create a "boss" character for a workplace series you were creating. TV series have had countless "boss" characters, and your temptation might be to merely imitate one of those. Bad idea. Your character would come off as exactly what it is — a pale imitation of somebody else's character. If, instead, you drew on real life — your own boss (you have a day job, surely) — well, then you've got a much better chance of creating a real character, an individual that seems like a flesh and blood human being, rather than a cardboard cutout. And even if your own real-life boss doesn't fit the bill, surely someone you know has a boss he's described in brutal detail who would fit the bill. My brother-in-law, for instance, once had a new boss come in on Day One and tell everyone that his goal was "to make sure that by Christmas time, the competition's children all had one less gift under the tree." Terrible, disgusting, repulsive boss. But great character — and memorable dialogue you'd never come up with on your own in a million years.

Growing Your Characters

The characters in your pilot are not intended to be a finished product. They are a work in progress. They must be, otherwise you will have nowhere to go in future episodes. For your series to continue to grow and thrive, your characters must do the same. And while much of this will be a voyage of discovery for you, and you will find ways for your characters to grow as you write and shoot more and more episodes and spend time with those characters, you should at least have some plans for how your characters will grow when you conceive your original series and character blueprint.

Character growth in a television series can be a tricky thing. On the one hand, the characters have to be consistent from week to week. Frasier must always be Frasier, from his first appearance in Season 3 of *Cheers* right through to his last appearance in Season 11 of his own series a full twenty years later. The same holds true for Codex, the Douche sisters, and Fiona Wallace, the inappropriate therapist and lead character in Lisa Kudrow's wonderful online comedy *Web Therapy*. But *consistent* should not be confused with *static*. Consistent means the character's core and essence — their attitudes and predominant ways of dealing with the world — remain the same. But the circumstances and challenges of their onscreen lives must evolve. Otherwise, the series will become repetitive and stale.

Think about the characters on the long-running network series *Friends*. Ross, Rachel, Chandler, Monica, Phoebe and Joey were recognizably the same characters from beginning to end. And yet their circumstances changed and evolved — new jobs, relationships, small increments of personal growth fueled by changes in the external circumstances around these characters.

That's how growth happens for series characters. Though they are essentially the same from episode to episode (consistent), they evolve in response to significant changes in their external world. This is why on network TV, as a series gets on in years, so many shows introduce new characters, new romances, or other major changes in the characters' lives, such as getting married or having children. It's a way to keep the characters — and the series — from stagnating and losing the audience.

So even though the main focus of your efforts (and this book) should be devoted to the pilot and the initial conceptualization of your series and characters, you should also have, in the back of your mind, at least some initial ideas about how the characters might grow or face new, life-changing challenges. Because web-only series are still in their infancy, there aren't as many to cite as examples on this front. But take *The Guild* again, now in its third season. Season 2 saw the introduction of Wade, Codex's hot, non-gamer neighbor. The introduction of an outsider to the gamer-obsessed world of Codex — especially a hot guy and potential love interest — puts further pressure on her character. In the series pilot, Codex gets dumped by her therapist for failing to acknowledge her video addiction. This new character potentially reawakens that challenge — but in a more compelling way because it comes from a hot guy.

One good way of thinking ahead about your characters' potential growth is to think in terms of season-long arcs. Characters A and B will butt heads all season long during Season 1 — but friction turns to sexual heat and they tumble into bed at the end of the last episode of Season 1. Now Season 2 can begin with a whole new energy and set of problems for your characters.

One note of caution on series growth: don't be tempted to "jump the shark." The phrase "jump the shark" refers to the last gasp of the series *Happy Days*. The show had essentially run out of gas — done everything they reasonably could to grow the characters and still perpetuate the premise. They probably should have made a graceful exit into the sunset while still on top in the ratings and creatively. But they tried to keep going and in the process stretched the premise beyond believability. For more than a decade, The Fonz had performed minor miracles — elbowing the dormant jukebox back to life and so on. But the "miracles" kept getting bigger — and bigger, and bigger. By Season 11, in an attempt to make The Fonz ever more heroic, they did an episode where The Fonz jumped a shark tank with his motorcycle. It was, to say the least, a ridiculous premise. The show had crossed the line from playful fantasy to the utterly absurd and unbelievable. And with that loss of believability came the loss of audience. They checked out. So yes, by all means, give your characters new challenges. But do not jump the shark. In your desire to be fresh and new, don't reach so far that you catapult your series right out if its own reality.

● FOR TEACHERS…

As with the previous chapter on premise, students can benefit from both analytical and creative assignments on character. For the analytical, have the students examine a current web series and dissect its characters and character landscape. They need to do more than merely summarize externals. They must identify the internal essence of each character, and then define how these characters create conflict and story potential by virtue of their conflicting and/or complimentary character traits.

The same sort of depth of thinking should transfer over to their creative presentation of the characters in their proposed series. They must define not just each character's individual qualities, but also how they work together — how each one plays off the other to create a rich and useful character landscape for the series. What type of story possibilities will there be between characters A and B? Character A and Character C? What about when B and D are together — what dynamics will that present?

CHAPTER FOUR
CREATING THE WORLD OF YOUR SERIES

When you create a television series you are not just coming up with a premise and a bunch of characters to populate that premise. You are creating an entire world, a coherent universe with its own rules, reality and gravity. That reality can be whatever you want it to be. It can be relatively ordinary, more or less like our own — America in the 21st century. Or it can be something entirely of your own making, an as yet undiscovered planet with its own unique and bizarre reality. This bizarre reality can even be right here, hidden in plain sight in the contemporary United States of America. Take the movie *Men In Black*, for instance — set in modern day New York City, but with a less than commonly accepted reality to its world — namely that aliens live among us and there is a government agency that patrols and monitors these beings. The "reality" and rules of the world you create for your series can be whatever you want. But — and this is a really big but, and I'm talking humongous, Rosie O'Donnell mega-booty — that reality must be consistent and true to itself at all times.

Laying Out The Rules

The rules of your series world can be plain and simple (e.g., it's ordinary, modern day

New York City exactly as we all know it), a slight alteration to commonly accepted reality (as in *Gaytown*, where the "rules" are that gay is the overwhelmingly dominant lifestyle and straights live closeted and imperiled lives), or it can involve a complex set of special rules that define the operation and behavior of a special world, say like in the movie *The Matrix*. But whatever the reality of your series, it must be consistent from episode to episode, and you must clearly define these rules for the audience early on in the series. Think about the movie *Men In Black* again. In the very first scene, they show you that aliens exist among us on this planet, that there is a special government agency that monitors these creatures, and that the knowledge that aliens live among us is such a closely guarded secret that even law enforcement officials (other than MIB) are kept in the dark. How are they and the rest of the population kept in the dark about this? The filmmakers show you, right in scene one. When the non-MIB officers witness alien behavior, they have their memories cleansed with a device called a neurolizer. The major rules of the *Men In Black* world are all laid out for the audience, right there in scene one. A few other particulars are knit in along the way, but the fundamentals are clearly defined right up front. This allows the audience to enjoy everything that follows without saying *Wait a minute, how come there are aliens but nobody knows about them?* If the audience starts asking those kinds of questions, or becomes confused by the rules of your world, they have been taken out of that world and can no longer enjoy it. Audiences are perfectly willing to "suspend disbelief" — to follow you into whatever universe you choose to create, no matter how wild and imaginative. In fact, they love it when you take them someplace they've never been before — just check out the box office stats for *Avatar*. But you have to give them a proper sense of gravity in your world by supplying them with a clear understanding of how that world operates.

Another note about rules: special rules don't always have to be about aliens or altered states of reality. Your world might be perfectly realistic — say the world of online gamers of *The*

Guild or the world of online therapy of *Web Therapy*. But these worlds require an explanation of "the rules" just as much as *Men In Black* or *Gaytown* do. Why? Because not everyone knows how online gaming or web-based therapy sessions work. So you have to explain the basics of these worlds to your audience — not by sending them a list of rules, or laying them out in a crawl at the top of your pilot, but by dramatizing and illustrating how these worlds work right in the body of your story.

So if the characters in *The Guild* are connected online via their game world, and are also connected by telephone and speak to each other over headsets while they interact online simultaneously, you need to show that. Same goes for *Web Therapy*. The therapist and her clients are not in the same room. They conduct their sessions via webcam, each in his/her own separate environment. You've got to show this early on for the audience to understand and enjoy your universe. This doesn't mean that you couldn't ever do an episode of *Web Therapy* where a client shows up at Fiona's office or house. It just means that you have to establish what the status quo of this world is on a normal day in order for the audience to understand that in this particular world, showing up to see the therapist face to face is a departure from the norm.

Reality vs. Believability

Fiction, whether it's a novel, movie, or an Internet television series, doesn't have to be one hundred percent real in a literal sense. It is, of course, made up by definition. But that doesn't mean that anything goes. Fiction does have to be believable. The audience has to be able to "go with the flow" of the reality you create. If that flow is interrupted by the audience having a *wait a minute, that's just not possible* moment, then you've lost them. You have violated the unspoken agreement between creator and audience — namely that they will follow you anywhere as long as the place you take them has a coherent reality to it. This world doesn't have to be factually authentic; it just has to *feel* authentic. It has to ring true on an emotional level.

Wait a minute moments happen primarily for two reasons. Reason One: the fantasy you've created is just so far-fetched or implausible that the audience is unable to "suspend disbelief" and accept your fictional universe. Reason Two: the rules seem inconsistent, or you suddenly or conveniently "forget" about one of the rules you've established in order to take the plot a certain direction.

Let's say you wanted to do a satire on presidential politics and our dysfunctional political process. To do this, you create a series where the American public, sick of both the Republicans and the Democrats, rejects both major candidates and overwhelmingly elects a family-sized jar of Claussen dill pickles as President of the United States. You can see the hilarious scenes in your head — CNN reporters on election night showing the vote tally with slides of the candidates: Barack Obama 8%, Sarah Palin 5%, the jar of pickles 87%. The Capitol steps on inauguration day with a record crowd of four million gathered to watch the historic swearing in of the brine-soaked veggies as leader of the free world. The Situation Room — with the Joint Chiefs of Staff solemnly asking the Pickle Jar in Chief whether they should invade Pakistan and waiting with bated breath as the jar just sits there at the head of the table. All hilarious in your mind. And it might even be worth a two-minute, one-time sketch on *Saturday Night Live* or *The Daily Show*. But I suspect if you tried this premise as the basis for an ongoing series, the audience would reject it as just flat-out impossible to believe.

Reason Two, violating the rules of your world as you have defined them, is equally deadly. To illustrate, let me use the feature film *The Firm*. The world of the film is that of a Memphis law firm with a special practice: they're the mob's law firm. Promising young lawyers (who look a lot like Tom Cruise) are brought into the firm as if it's just an ordinary, legitimate practice, given a taste of the good life, and then told the truth about who they work for and informed that if they try to leave or talk to the feds, they and their loved ones will be killed. The senior partners and their henchmen watch your every move: they bug your house, your car, they even keep track of how and when you use the copy machine. Young Tom is taken on a business trip to the Cayman Islands by senior partner Gene Hackman. Cruise shows up at Hackman's firm-owned condo to go to dinner. Hackman, still getting dressed in the bedroom, tells Cruise to help himself to some snacks and that the key to the cabinet is on the key ring right there on the kitchen counter. Cruise picks up the keys, opens the wrong closet, and, lo and behold, right there staring him in the face are boxes and boxes of secret firm billing records, all conveniently labeled "Shit That Could Send Us to Prison 1984-88." Well now — that's just not consistent with the reality they had set up and it took me right out of the movie. The movie asks me to believe that the mob — which conducts surveillance of everything right down to your underwear — keeps its secret, incriminating records in a closet with no armed guard, no video cameras, and the key to the closet is on the same key ring as the key to the honor bar. Please.

Building On The Reality You Create

Just as you will want your series characters to grow and evolve, you may also want to grow and evolve the overall world you create in your series. Expanding your series universe is often a key to keeping a long-running series fresh and vital. Sometimes this expansion is merely a matter of adding a new character or two. But series evolution can also mean expanding or modifying the rules or parameters of your series universe.

Let's use the classic network sitcom *Cheers* as an example. For the first five years of the series, one of the "rules" was that Sam was the boss. It was his bar. But going into year six, with the departure of the Diane character, played by Shelley Long, the show's producers knew they needed to add a new female antagonist to play against Sam. And they didn't want this new female to have the exact same relationship to Sam as Diane did. That would be a backwards step for the show, not growth. So they solved their problem by not only adding a new, attractive female to the cast, but by altering the series rule that Sam was in charge. When Season 6 began, Kirstie Alley joined the cast as Rebecca Howe. And she was Sam's boss — hired to manage the bar by the company Sam had sold it to. This new dynamic gave the series fresh stories and angles to explore. It meant Sam had to answer to a woman, perhaps for the first time in his life. It added jeopardy to Sam's situation — which added fresh comedy and drama.

Adding fresh angles to your series can and should be a part of your long-range planning for it. You don't even have to know what all of them will be. Nobody knows exactly what will happen in Episode 10 or 27 or 57 when they write a pilot, not even the creators of highly serialized material like *Sam Has 7 Friends* or the Fox network thriller *24*. TV series, and the characters in them, somehow have a life of their own. Each script you write and episode you shoot will spawn new ideas in your mind about where to take them and the show. Being open to these new ideas is crucial to keeping your show fresh and vital. Again, you can't suddenly make a change so radical that it feels like a wholesale violation of the rules of gravity you've created. But you can and should be open to the natural evolution that comes from working with a premise and characters over time, and you must strive to introduce new wrinkles from time to time. Introducing new elements and dynamics makes your series universe seem more believable and "alive." In real life, unexpected new obstacles are a daily occurrence. Change happens, and that's a good thing. The same should be true for the fictional world you create, because if it's exactly the same episode after episode, your audience will click elsewhere and make the big change themselves, effectively cancelling your series.

● FOR TEACHERS...

Though it is highly doubtful that your students will be any more accurate in predicting exactly how their series will develop than we professionals are, it is still valuable to make them think about where their series could go in the future. It will help them conceive of their premise and characters as dynamic and alive, rather than fixed and static.

As an exercise, have your students write a one-paragraph pitch for potential episodes 10, 20 and 30. In addition to the plot for each episode, they should explain how that particular episode and story will help to grow one or more of the characters and make the series richer to explore.

CHAPTER FIVE
THE PILOT – STORY

Okay, so now you've studied the landscape of Internet TV shows and know it inside and out, and have a dynamite premise for your own short-form series that has a compelling hook and legs like Angelina Jolie. You've got a great lead character, wonderful supporting characters, and know more about the tone and rules of your series idea than the Desperate Housewives know about botox. Time to sit down and write the pilot script, right?

Wrong! You're still missing one vital element before you can write the script. To paraphrase that commercial about baby boomers heading toward retirement — *you, my friend, you need a plan.* And when it comes to planning a script, the basic plan or blueprint you need is the story or outline for your pilot episode.

You might be asking, *haven't I already done that*? No, you have not. Coming up with a premise and characters for a series is not the same as planning the story for the pilot. The premise and characters tell us what the series will be like on an ongoing basis; they define the shape of the series week after week. That's why you have to develop them first. But now the task is to figure out how you will specifically introduce that premise and those characters in one episode — the first episode or pilot for your series.

Creating A Pilot Story That *Tells* And *Sells*

Just like the title of your series, your pilot story must *tell* and *sell*. It must tell your audience what the show is about, and make them want to watch more episodes. It must also introduce your regular series characters, serve as a template for all future episodes, define the tone and style of your series (which you will consistently adhere to in all future episodes), and tell its own unique, self-contained story that both promises dozens of stories to come and is satisfying and interesting in and of itself.

The biggest "rookie mistake" my students make when pitching their pilot story is that they construct it to introduce the premise and characters — but nothing else. The story sets the basic gears of the concept in motion, sets up the premise, but doesn't serve as an illustration of what a typical future episode will be like. The pilot episode must do both. Is that a lot to ask? You bet. But you're creating an entire world, and that takes time, effort and skill.

Premise Pilot vs. 'Episode 10' Pilot

The first decision you need to make in devising your pilot story is whether you are going to do a "premise pilot" or an "Episode 10" pilot. A premise pilot is one where the plot and action of the pilot episode are necessary in order to create the basic series situation not just for the audience, but for the characters within the series. If the premise of your series is best explained by showing those characters at the moment they are thrown into an entirely new life situation, then that calls for a premise pilot. An Episode 10 pilot is one where the basic situation of the series is already in place for the characters, and we, the audience, have just chosen this particular moment to drop in on their lives. The events of the pilot are not a drastic change in circumstances for the characters. We merely pick up their story "in progress."

An example of a premise pilot from network television would be *Step By Step*, a show about a blended family where the parents love each other but the kids do constant battle. The creators chose to begin the series by showing the two families as they get together during the pilot, as opposed to having them already living as one family. Why? Because having the situation be new to everyone increased the conflict and number of stories that could be told within the basic premise. It also made it easier to write exposition and backstory. Because the characters themselves were new to each other and the situation, we got to learn about it right alongside them, rather than them having to "casually" say things that they already knew just so we, the audience, could catch up with the information.

Seinfeld, on the other hand, chose to introduce the series with an Episode 10 pilot. Why? Because that show required that the characters already know each other well in order to tell the kind of stories they wanted to in the tone they envisioned. The series was built on the concept that these four people had a history together. If Jerry, George, Elaine and Kramer were just meeting each other for the first time in the pilot, it would have been impossible to tell stories based on casual intimacy and long-term knowledge of each other's foibles and shortcomings.

There is one other type of pilot story: a hybrid of the premise pilot and Episode 10 approaches. In a hybrid pilot story, most of the characters are already living the lives and relationships they will continue to live in the series, but one or two new characters or elements are introduced to the pre-existing world. The pilot for the classic NBC sitcom *Cheers* utilized this technique. Sam Malone, the womanizing owner of the bar, was already there, as were Carla the sharp-tongued waitress, Sam's former major league baseball mentor Coach (who had taken one too many fastballs to the head), and bar regulars Norm and Cliff. But the pilot introduced one major new character to the group — snooty intellectual Diane — who shows up at the bar expecting to marry her college professor beau, only to be dumped, humiliated and left in the bar without a love life or a future — whereupon Sam offers

her a job at the bar, and the unspoken but unmistakable promise of romantic tension and eventual consummation between the
two of them.

If the premise you devise calls for most of the characters
having pre-established relationships, with one or more new
characters introduced into that established world, then a hybrid
approach might be best for your pilot story.

Choosing which type of pilot story to pursue comes down
to one basic question: which form best serves your particular
premise?

You've Only Got A Few Minutes, So Be Economical

Because pilots have to accomplish so much — introduce all the
characters and the basic situation, tell a satisfying story, set up
future episodes, etc. — they can be quite daunting to write —
even more so when you are creating a short-form series and only
have a few minutes to tell, sell and entertain. How can you possibly write one little five-minute script that does all that? First
of all (hopefully), you've started with a premise that is easy to
understand and simple to convey, and with a small enough set
of core characters that they can fit comfortably into the limited
space of the short-form Internet format. If, on the other hand,
what you have in mind is a set of stories about a planet five hundred years in the future, where humans do battle with eleven
distinct and previously unknown forms of life, and each of these
life forms will have some characters who are good guys, some
who are villains, and some who shift back and forth, bringing
the total number of core characters to sixty or seventy, and in
addition to being a science fiction vehicle it also contains seven
intersecting love stories, as well as flashbacks and flash forwards
to other planets in other periods of time — well then perhaps
this premise would be better served in a form other than the five-
minute web series — say, perhaps, a 5,000-page graphic novel.

But let's assume for the moment that you haven't lost your mind and have developed an appropriately compact premise with one to five core characters. Even then, you've got a lot on your plate in devising a successful and entertaining pilot. If you hope to accomplish everything you must in just a few minutes, you will need to be economical. So the first question you should ask yourself is *does the audience need to know about all five of these characters in the very first episode or can I hold off introducing one or more of them until Episode 2?* In the world of half-hour and one-hour shows, it's generally a rule that you have to use every series regular in every single episode, including the pilot. But web TV doesn't have to be a slave to the old rules. If you've got two main characters and three supporting ones, and the heart of your show is the two main characters and their interaction, maybe your show will be better served introducing the two main characters and one supporting character in the pilot, then introducing the other two recurring characters in Episodes 2 and 3, or even later.

The next task on the road to economy is devising a pilot that tells us the most important things we need to know about the central characters and their situation in the most efficient and memorable way possible. Notice I didn't say tells us *everything* about the characters and situation. You can't possibly tell the audience everything they will want or need to know. If you could, you wouldn't have any more stories to tell or episodes to write and it would be the end of your series. But you do need to tell us the fundamental, crucial things we need to know in order to understand who and what your show is about. You may know fifty things about your main character's traits and background. But which one or two are the MOST important for us to know, the MOST central to establishing the essence of who that character is and the basic premise of your series? To return to the case of *Cheers*, the most important things for us to know about Sam and Diane were that he was a womanizing ex-jock and recovering alcoholic who ran the bar and she was a smug intellectual who had just been dumped by another smug intellectual. That's all the audience needs to know from the pilot in order to say, *oooh, and they're attracted to each other, what's gonna happen when they get together*?

Once you've decided which characters must be introduced and what essentials we must know about them, your job is figuring out how to introduce them in the most memorable way possible. What can they say or do to instantly burn an indelible image of those characters in the mind of the audience?

Creating Memorable Character Introductions

One of the best character introductions I know is the opening scene of the film *All That Jazz*, where we meet the film's main character, Broadway director/choreographer Joe Gideon. Gideon's defining traits are that he is a workaholic on a collision course with death through glib self-destruction. The film opens with his morning routine — hung over, popping amphetamines, showering with a cigarette still dangling from his lips. He looks in the mirror, puts on a false face of joy and exclaims, "It's showtime!" In a matter of mere seconds, we know the most important things we need to about Joe Gideon and his life of cheery self-destruction.

While it doesn't have to be the first scene in your pilot, you should strive to create a story that contains vivid moments for each of your core characters that unforgettably tell us exactly who they are. It might be an action or image (such as smoking the cigarette in the shower) or it could be dialog. Think Clint Eastwood as Dirty Harry, hovering over a criminal thinking about reaching for his gun — Harry's finger poised on the trigger of his .44 Magnum as he growls, "Feel lucky, punk?"

That's the kind of high-impact, memorable character introduction you should strive for in your pilot — indelible snapshots that capture the essence of each character. Watch the pilot episode of *Be a Celebutante*. You'll know in less than thirty seconds exactly who these rich, shallow, spoiled women are. Same goes for *The Ed Hardy Boyz* — clear and instant creation of vivid main characters.

Story Structure: Beginning-Middle-End

Endless volumes have been written dissecting the "hidden secrets" of story structure. The more academic and wordy of these tomes seem to suggest that telling a story is as complex a task as building a nuclear reactor, requiring decades of study, a team of internationally trained physicists, and a secret stash of Uranium 235. I don't want to suggest that any idiot can tell a story — storytelling at its best is an art. But the basics of story structure are as simple as this: every story has a beginning, a middle, and an end, and each of these parts has a specific set of functions it must fulfill.

Though that last sentence may seem entirely self-evident (*every story has a beginning, a middle, and an end... duh!*), it's really quite a useful tool — but *only* if you remember to include the second part of the sentence — *each of these parts has a specific set of functions it must fulfill.*

We'll start, naturally, with the **beginning**. The beginning of all stories — including short-form web pilots — has three main jobs. Job One — introduce the main character(s). If the script for your webisode pilot is six pages long, but we don't meet your main character until page four, then you don't have a properly structured beginning to your story. In that example, we don't even know who the story is about until it's almost over. Mistake. Big mistake. Start over and rethink the story structure. The beginning is roughly the first twenty to thirty percent of your story. You have to let us know who the main character of your story is during that time.

If Job One of the beginning of your story can be described as **who**, then Job Two might be described as **what** — what is the basic situation for your main character, and what happens early in your story to upset the status quo, giving your main character a new problem or situation he must respond to and act upon? Let's return to the pilot episode of *The Guild*. Right off the bat we meet Codex (**who**), a young woman whose therapist fires her because she has an online gaming addiction she refuses to acknowledge (the status quo part of **what** plus a bit of a new problem). Soon thereafter, fellow online gamer Zaboo shows up at Codex's apartment, convinced they are destined for each other. That's the central problem of the pilot story — this guy has invaded her space and is now pursuing her like a lovesick techno-geek stalker. Simple, clear, economical and efficient — a good solid structure for a beginning.

The final component of a strong beginning — Job Three — is that "world of the story" stuff we talked about. In order for the audience to fully understand the main character and his or her central problem, you must also let the audience know what world they are dealing with. Ordinary? Gaming addicts? Spoiled celebrity heiresses? Aliens with supernatural powers? That, too, is a crucial part of the what.

At this point you may find yourself thinking *how the hell am I supposed to get all that into the first page and a half of a five-page script?* It can, indeed, seem an impossible mountain to climb. But the key in the short-form webisode world is boiling the story and situation down to its essence and not getting bogged down in a million details or side journeys that, interesting as they may be, are better suited to a longer storytelling form. Think about the ultra-short story form commonly known as jokes. *Guy walks into a bar* — five words and already I know **who** and the first part of **what**, the basic situation. *Guy walks into a bar with a duck on his head* — now I know the full story of **what** — this guy's main problem. All in a matter of seconds. Yes, I know, you want to tell a real story, not some lame joke. Fair enough. But you're also not writing *War And Peace*, or even *Harold And Kumar Go To White Castle*. If you can't think of a way to economically introduce the main character of your web series and his or her central problem in two pages, then think some more. If you wrack your brains for days and come to the conclusion that it will take at least ten pages to introduce even the most rudimentary version of the who and what of your series, then your premise isn't suitable to the short-form Internet format. Use the idea for something else — a 30- or 60-minute network pilot spec, or even a feature film — and work on coming up with another idea that does fit the extreme demands for economy of this compact story form.

The basic function of the middle can be boiled down to two words: **complications** and **escalations**. Your beginning has introduced your main character, his normal world, and the new problem he must contend with. The middle is all about dealing with that problem. Your main character, like all of us, will naturally try the simplest, easiest way to solve that problem (Codex asks Zaboo to leave). But of course that first, easy solution won't work for your hero so he'll have to try harder. That's the essence of the middle — making things even more difficult and more complicated for your main character. Things have to get worse for your hero during the middle. If the new problem your hero encounters in the beginning section of your pilot story is that his mother-in-law, whom he despises, is coming to stay for a month, the next problem can't be that the shirt he wanted to wear isn't clean. That's not an escalation, a bigger problem, it's a backward step to a smaller problem — unless the shirt was a gift from the mother-in-law and she expects him to wear it and he must now either wear it crumpled and dirty (and get shit for that) or not wear it (even more shit). If the beginning introduces a hateful mother-in-law coming to visit for a month, then the middle must escalate or complicate things — she decides to move in forever, say, or your central couple finds out that his mother has decided to come stay with them for a month as well.

You might at this point find yourself saying *but I'm not exactly telling a narrative story, I'm doing humor, so it's just a bunch of funny things that happen to my main character.* You still need to have a beginning-middle-end to your pilot (and your episodes) and there must be an escalation or build to the middle. In the case of broad comedy, that escalation or build means the humorous situations your character finds himself in must get progressively funnier or more outrageous. If not — if you start with your funniest bit and things get less funny from there — your audience will tune out and click away in dissatisfaction.

This doesn't mean you start with something weak. It means you need to start strong and get even stronger.

Here's an example from the feature film world of how escalation is crucial to comedy. In the movie *American Pie*, there is a scene where the main teen boy's father decides to talk to him about sex. The father is determined to have this discussion despite the fact that his son would rather die than talk to dad about sex. Things get worse when dad breaks out a series of magazines to aid the discussion. The magazines the father pulls out of his brown bag are — in this order — *Playboy*, *Hustler*, and a magazine called *Shaved*. That's escalation. The magazines get progressively raunchier. Each is a distinct step up in how uncomfortable it makes the son. If, on the other hand, dad started with *Penthouse*, then *Hustler* would be more of a duplication than an escalation. And the scene would have no comic build to it.

Okay, so comedy or drama, narrative or sketch, you will have a beginning that introduces your central character and his problem, and a middle that elevates and heightens that problem. By the end of the middle — or the beginning of the **end**, if you prefer — that escalation will reach a **crisis and climax.** This is the make or break point of your pilot episode where the main characters must sink or swim. In the *Cheers* pilot, it's Sam's job offer to Diane. Will she swallow her pride, take this waitress job that is, in her mind, degradingly beneath her? If she does take it, is it because she really has nowhere else to turn — or because she's attracted to Sam? In action stories, this crisis and climax is usually "the big shootout." The race to blow up the Death Star in *Star Wars*, or pistols at twenty paces at high noon in a western. In a romantic comedy in series format, it's the moment when our two heroes commit to being with each other (see *Cheers* again) or are locked into being with each other against their will so that we can enjoy their love/hate antics going forward. In a broad comedy, this is (hopefully) the "big joke" — the funniest bit in the whole episode. It doesn't always work this way — sometimes audiences pick something from the middle as their favorite joke. But this final joke or bit better be in the top three.

The final portion of the **end** — after your crisis and climax — is the **resolution**. How does your story end? Where do you leave the characters? And what problems do you leave them with going forward? In self-contained stories — a novel, or a feature film — this resolution usually leaves us with the feeling that problems have been solved and a new status quo is in place. It's a return to calm. This is frequently the case in ordinary episodes of TV and Internet series as well. But a pilot is a different animal. It must leave the audience with both a sense of satisfaction with this one episode, your pilot, *and* a sense that this is merely the beginning, a sense that many more stories about these characters in this situation have yet to be told. Sam and Diane will be working together — so now what? Zaboo just won't get out of Codex's apartment, so now what? It may seem a contradiction, but a well-crafted pilot ends with the sense that things have only just begun. You must leave your audience begging for more. Like another type of climax and aftermath, you want your partner (in this case, the audience) to be utterly, blissfully satisfied — and eager as hell to do it all over again and again and again.

Putting It On Paper — Creating An Outline

One of the main differences between professionals and amateurs in the film and video world is that professionals don't skip steps. Professionals know there is discipline and value in each step along the way — developing the concept and characters first, then writing an outline for the story, then writing a draft of the script. Amateurs are so excited by their raw ideas, so enthralled by their possibilities, and so eager to fulfill the dream of seeing these ideas on the screen that they often jump right from the moment of inspiration to grabbing a camera, rounding up some props and actors, and shooting it right then and there. This is a recipe for failure. It's usually about as successful as getting the inspiration *I want a steak* and simply grabbing the nearest hunk of raw red meat and chomping into it. Raw meat isn't a steak. It has to be properly prepared first — seasoned, then cooked — in order for it to achieve its full potential.

The same goes for your series idea and pilot for it. The raw ingredients — the premise and characters and rough idea for the story — must be carefully, methodically prepared before they are served. If you skip any part of the process — including putting your story outline down on paper in prose form before you fire up your screenplay formatting software (more on that in the next chapter), you run the risk of ruining a perfectly good raw ingredient — namely your story idea. The reason is that your mind can play tricks on you. In your mind, that flash of inspiration for your series and pilot feels like a vivid, complete rendering of the idea. You can *see it* already, unspooling in sound and image on the flat-screen monitor in your mind. I believe you. Happens to me all the time. That's how you get excited about creating — that unpredictable, elusive moment when the idea for something first pops into your head. But experience has taught me that this moment, thrilling as it is, is only a first step. If I go from raw idea and just start typing a script, no matter how vivid that idea seemed in my head, I always crash and burn very quickly. You have to be disciplined and put the story outline on paper first. Because when you force yourself to put the story on paper, you start seeing all the holes in your idea that the leprechaun of creation in your brain, manic magician that he is, managed to gloss over in his fevered excitement. This can be a discouraging moment. The leprechaun is shouting *this is great, it'll be great, let's shoot it!* But a calmer voice — perhaps one that resembles one of your high school teachers, usually the one in charge of training the hall monitors, is gently urging you to look before you leap. Most of us would rather be leprechauns than hall monitors. But the hall monitor part of us, geeky party pooper that he may seem to be, is doing us a favor. He's saying slow down, think this through, and make this story the best it can be. So write it down — tell your story to yourself in prose form, on paper, scene by scene. Then read it over and pretend you are seeing it for the first time. I know — that's impossible. But try. Evaluate it as if it were someone else telling you a story. Is the premise of the series clear based on the outline you read? Are the characters sharply and clearly defined? Does the story have a clear beginning, middle and end? With a clear central problem that escalates to a crisis, climax and resolution? And finally, when you get to the end of the story, does it leave you wanting to see more episodes? If the answer to any of these questions is no — or even something tepid like "kind of" — then do not pass Go. Do not begin writing your script, thinking you'll fix it then. Take the time to consider how you can turn that "no" or "kind of" into a resounding "absolutely" right now, here, in the outline phase.

Pitch It Out Loud To A Friend Or Three

Now that you feel you have a solid story outline, there is one more checkpoint to pass through before you write the actual script. You need to test your idea on a few people. The best way to do this is to pitch your series idea and pilot story to them — out loud. This provides several benefits. First, when you tell someone else your idea and story, it will quickly become obvious to you whether it makes sense or not outside of your own head. Either they get it or they don't. If the people you pitch to all have a blank stare on their faces, or a look of utter confusion, then you need to rework either your concept or your pilot story. They're not getting it. Or if they're smiling and following along, clearly enjoying it, then go blank in one particular scene, you need to examine what's wrong with that scene.

Next, after you pitch to them, ask them what they think. This does not mean you are turning over creative control of your idea to these people. Merely that you are soliciting their reactions. If they all react the same way — for instance, if they all say the ending isn't satisfying, or they all feel they need more backstory about your characters in order to understand who they are

— then you should consider how to address this universal point of confusion for your audience. If, on the other hand, they each have different ideas about what they like or don't like, then you have to decide for yourself whether their suggestions are worth incorporating or not.

Finally, a word about who you choose to pitch to and get feedback from. Do not choose people who are by nature bitter, critical, or derive joy from crushing the spirit of those around them. This does not mean you should only pitch to those who will mindlessly kiss up to you and say what a genius you are. You want honest, thoughtful criticism. But the last thing you need is a committed naysayer who thinks all ideas suck except their own.

It is also important that you pitch to people who might be part of the intended audience for your pilot. If it is aimed at college students, your 70-year-old neighbor, even if he won several Emmys for his work on a groundbreaking ABC miniseries in the 1970s, may not be the right test audience. So pick several people who enjoy shows like the one you have in mind. They don't even have to be writers or filmmakers. They just need to be people who like watching short-form videos on the Web and fit the basic parameters of the audience you imagine might be interested in your show.

● FOR TEACHERS...

The pilot story phase is one where many students begin to crash and burn. This is because, while they may have great raw ideas, they are often lacking in the craft and skills required to tell a story, compounded by the fact that this particular form puts such a heavy demand on craft due to its ferocious need for economy.

Guide them gently but firmly through this phase. MAKE THEM PUT THEIR STORY PITCH OR OUTLINE ON PAPER. Then discuss it with them, scene by scene. Give them the benefit of your greater experience here. Point out potential trouble spots. If you are reading an outline of a scene that reads like a four-page scene to you, press them on that point. Ask them how they plan to convey all the action and information the outline suggests in such a limited amount of space.

One other thing here — don't be afraid to make them start over with their story. If their story just doesn't work, writing the script itself will be a waste of time. Guide them, help them, make sure that they have at least the basics of a solid pilot story in place before letting them go to script.

CHAPTER SIX
THE PILOT – SCRIPT

Now that you've got a solid story outline for your pilot episode, it's time to turn that outline into a script — a short screenplay. While an outline is written in standard prose as a narrative, a script is written in screenplay format. (For a simple tutorial on proper screenplay format, see Appendix 1.)

There are several reasons why screenplays are formatted the way they are. First and foremost, a script is meant to be filmed, so a screenplay is not only a means to conveying a story, it must also serve as a blueprint for shooting a film. That's why it contains elements like:

```
EXT. PLAYGROUND — DAY

MARIE (early 30s) watches COLE (5)
as he blows soap bubbles into the
air by the swing set.
```

The people who plan the filming of the script (in the case of your web series, that means YOU) need to identify each location (here, a playground), whether it is a day scene or night scene, who's in the scene, what props will be needed, etc. Screenplay format facilitates the process by which these crucial production elements can be spotted, highlighted, and tracked.

The second benefit of screenplay format is that in a film, the only information the audience can receive is what they see (the actions, movements and facial expressions of the actors or physical objects) and what they hear (dialogue, sound effects, music.) Thus, while a prose piece can contain what is known as "interior monologue" — spelling out what one or more characters are thinking — a screenplay can only communicate a character's internal thoughts through external means; i.e., what he says or does. A script's primary components aren't paragraphs, but segments of action and of dialogue.

The third reason scripts are written in this special form is that screenplay format helps the reader translate the written word more directly into sounds and images, elements that enable him to "see a movie" — visualize the action and dialogue as they will appear on screen. Consider the following:

```
EXT. HARD BODIES STRIP CLUB — DAY

A jumbo jet on its final approach roars past
a sign that reads "Live Nude Girlz." An aging
Volvo station wagon sputters into the Hard Bodies
parking lot. PROFESSOR ROSS BROWN (54) steps out
of the Volvo, pulls a baseball cap down low over
his eyes, crosses to the club's entrance. He
throws a nervous glance over his shoulder as he
slinks into the club.
```

You see a shot from a movie, right? Several shots, probably — an establishing shot of a strip club near an airport, followed by a shot of a car pulling into the parking lot and a middle-aged man stepping out of the car and entering the club in an uneasy manner. In a novel the same scene might be handled like this:

```
The first thing Professor Brown noticed as he
pulled into the parking lot of Hard Bodies was
the sickening stench of jet fuel. Through the
dusty windshield of his aging Volvo he watched
a jet glide past the "Live Nude Girlz" sign. He
slapped on a baseball cap and prayed that nobody
he knew would spot him as he hurried to the
front door and into the club.
```

That description, while it conveys the same basic information as the screenplay format version, is not suitable for a script. Why not? Because people in a movie theater don't get scratch-'n'-sniff cards with jet fuel stench on them. Neither can they read the professor's mind to know that he hopes nobody spots him. So make sure in your script that you focus on what we can see or hear. If you want us to know something internal or unseen, such as what a character thinks or feels, then you must do that through dialogue or specific actions that communicate those internal musings to the audience in a tangible visual or audible way.

Building Your Script, Scene By Scene

Just as your overall story has a beginning, middle and end, each individual scene is its own mini-story, with the same beginning-middle-end rhythm to it. Your outline tells you *what* the story of each scene is. But now that you are turning that story into a fully realized script, you need to take that scene and decide *how* to tell it, as its own self-contained little story. You will need to decide: How much of the scene will be told through action vs. how much will be told through dialogue? Which pieces of the story will be revealed in what order? Is there a more effective way to tell the same story? Are there actions that can dramatize the point of the scene more memorably than dialogue? A thousand little decisions go into shaping not just the broad concept of your series and the construction of your pilot story, but the crafting and construction of each individual scene.

Let's go back to our scene of Professor Brown pulling into the parking lot of the strip club. I chose to tell that little mini-story by focusing on the setting first:

```
EXT. HARD BODIES — DAY

A jumbo jet on its final approach roars past a
sign that reads "Live Nude Girlz."
```

But I could have made another choice: I could have focused the audience's attention not on the setting, but on the character, like this:

```
EXT. PARKING LOT — NIGHT

PROFESSOR ROSS BROWN (54) nervously eyes his
surroundings. He starts to get out of his aging
Volvo, then stops, grabs a baseball cap, and
pulls it down as far as he can, hiding half his
face.

ANOTHER ANGLE

Professor Brown emerges from the car, slinks
across the parking lot into a club called Hard
Bodies, whose marquee reads "Live Nude Girlz."
```

There is no one answer as to which version is better. It depends in part on intangible elements like personal taste, and in part on the context — what came before this scene. Have we already met Professor Brown or is this our introduction to him? If we've never met him before, I'd probably opt for Version #1 — setting the scene, then introducing the person in that scene — because the location tells us at least something about this unknown person we are meeting for the first time. If, on the other hand, the previous scene was of Professor Brown teaching a philosophy class, delivering a lecture on morality and personal choices, I'd probably opt for Version #2. Why? Because the previous scene, the morality lecture, would prepare the audience for the parking lot scene. We can cut directly to the closer shot of the professor in his car, clearly about to do something that makes him uneasy. We, the audience, have context for his nervousness. We're already thinking *he's about to do something he doesn't feel right about, something morally questionable*. This creates suspense — we want to know what it is that the professor is about to do — and suspense engages the audience, makes them sit forward in their seats and say *I wonder what's going to happen next*. By holding off the reveal — that he's about to go into a sleazy strip club — the audience is drawn into the character and his situation more effectively than if you showed the club first, then showed the professor's nervousness.

Notice that this one tiny little scene is less than a quarter of a page in each version and yet, as the writer, you must make a string of important decisions. Should I start with the setting or the character? How will I show that the professor is nervous about being seen? How much of a "disguise" will he use? *A moustache?* No — too ridiculous. *A ski cap?* It's July in Los Angeles, why would he have a ski cap in his car? Even the tiny decision to spell the word *Girlz* on the marquee with a "z" rather than an "s" is a conscious decision, meant to convey the cheesiness of the setting and the character's action.

The point is that, in going from outline to screenplay, you are not merely reformatting from prose to screen format. You are also changing storytelling mediums and must now carefully consider the best, most effective way to take a story built from sentences and paragraphs — your outline — and turn it into a story built from sounds and images. This must be done with each and every scene. How do you go about making this conversion from prose to screenplay? First you read the scene as it is in your outline. Then, try to imagine it as you'd like to see the scene on a movie screen. What do you see or hear as you imagine it? Don't rush to answer this question. Give your creative mind the chance to take the raw material and work with it. Even though you may think you know exactly what the scene is from your outline, writing is a process where each step of the way — premise, then characters, then story outline, then script — adds and refines. New elements spring into your mind that you hadn't imagined before, elements that modify and strengthen your original thoughts and images. Maybe when you built your outline, your entire description of the scene was *Professor Brown pulls into the parking lot of a sleazy strip club.* Simple, clean and effective — perfectly good for an outline. But now, as you sit at your keyboard and imagine the movie version of that scene, your challenge is to give the audience tangible cinematic evidence of *sleazy* — visual cues that characterize the setting for the movie audience the same way the adjective *sleazy* did for the reading audience. Those visual cues, in my script version, are the signs that read "Hard Bodies" and "Live Nude Girlz," and the proximity to the airport.

You must go through this thoughtful process of translating prose into cinematic action and dialogue scene by scene by scene. The devil is in the details, and the details that take the bones of a story (your outline) and turn it into a fleshed-out screenplay (basis for a short movie) take time, thought and effort. Don't rush. Take your time as you imagine, write, rewrite and improve your story and turn it into a script.

One other note: economy is of the essence. Your entire story will be perhaps five minutes in length. You can't spend the first ninety seconds setting up the atmosphere for Scene One. Chose your details with precision. Give us the key elements, the ones that speak volumes about the character and situation, and then keep the action moving forward.

Deviating From The Outline

It's inevitable. No matter how much time you've spent developing your premise, constructing your characters, and working and reworking the story for your pilot, when you sit down and begin to actually write the script, you will want to change some things. New ideas will spring to mind — not just added details, but substantive differences. In the outline of the story about Professor Brown, perhaps you simply imagined the parking lot scene, then figured you'd cut right to the professor having dinner with his wife and children. But now, as you are imagining the parking lot scene and the professor nervously glancing over his shoulder to see if anyone sees him going into the club, you begin to think about that notion. *Wouldn't it be more powerful if someone he knows does see him? And wouldn't it be stronger if he's seen not just in the parking lot, but inside the club itself?* You start getting excited about this new thought and begin to imagine the professor inside the club. Who might see him? In a flash it comes to you: *Oh! Oh! I know! It's one of his students. A guy from the philosophy class. No, wait — better yet, it's a girl... and she's one of the dancers!*

Does this mean you "got it wrong" in the outline and should have thought of this back then? No — it's just part of the process. And now that you have this new idea about seeing the female student working the pole in the club, you'll naturally want to go back to the classroom scene and make sure you "set her up" — establish her and her reaction to the morality lecture in that scene so we know who she is in the strip club scene. Maybe you'll want to add dialogue — a question she asks the professor, or perhaps you'll merely want to write in a shot of her facial reaction. In either case, your one new idea — adding an interior of the club scene where the professor sees a female student working there and she sees him — necessitates one or more changes to the previous scene. THIS IS ALL GOOD! This is how writing and creativity build upon themselves.

To be perfectly honest, as I was writing this chapter, I merely thought I'd use the parking lot scene as a concrete visual example for the previous section, on turning a prose outline into a screenplay. But as I began writing this section, I realized I could get more out of the example by using it for this section as well. That's the creative mind at work. It builds things layer by layer.

Does this mean you should blindly follow your creative mind wherever it wanders? Absolutely not. Sometimes your creative mind is so wildly manic and inventive that it leads you completely off track, away from the core of the story you are telling. When that happens, you must remind your beloved creative mind that not every impulse it has is a good or useful one.

Every writer must balance creativity with discipline. I always picture this partnership as if I'm wearing a double-sided baseball cap, like those Sherlock Holmes hats with two brims, one in front, and one in back. The front of the cap says CREATOR. It's the front because the creator, the one who has the initial inspiration, gets to go first. But then I have to flip the cap around to the other side, the one that says EDITOR. This is the analytical part of my writer self, the one that must honestly assess my raw creative ideas and distinguish the useful ones (the ones that further the story I'm telling, tell it more vividly, or tell the audience more about the characters) from the ideas that either clutter the story, change the characters in a bad way, or are distractions or detours away from my core story.

Sometimes this battle between your creative self and your disciplined/analytical self can be difficult. The creative self runs on adrenaline and pure excitement and can tend to see the editor part of your brain as some sort of evil hall monitor bent on enforcing petty rules that spoil all the fun. But you — the complete writer — need both the creator and the editor if you are to do the best possible job on the project all three of you are working on. So remind yourself that all three of you — your creative self, your editorial self and your complete writer self — have to play nicely together and treat each other with respect. Your editor will save your ass a million times, stopping your hyperactive creator from wandering off into the woods. But your creative self is not subservient to the editor; he is an equal partner. The creator is the only one who can help you rise beyond the ordinary and boring to tell a truly exciting and vivid story.

It can be tricky business, this task of balancing your creative and editorial impulses. But hey, if you want to write and to make movies, then you better learn to embrace the tricky and the complex. If you crave simple, then repeat after me: *Would you like fries with that?*

What Makes Good Dialogue — The "4 Cs"

Great dialogue is an art all its own. At its best, dialogue pushes the story forward, characterizes the speaker and perhaps the person he's talking about, disseminates facts the audience needs to understand the plot, captures a perfect sense of the times and environment of the script, and somehow seems to do all of this effortlessly and naturally, as if the lines spoken by the actors are the only ones that could ever have been written.

This effortlessness, of course, is an illusion. Dialogue is crafted with the same care and attention to detail that you put into your story. It is molded, shaped, reshaped and refined many times over. The trick is making it *seem* natural and effortless. This is a complex task, one that takes a great deal of practice to truly master. But boiled down to its essence, good dialogue must fulfill what I call the "4 Cs." It must be:

- In **Character**
- **Concise**
- **Connective**
- **Clear**

Sounds simple enough, right? Yes and no. Let's take a closer look at the process involved in achieving the 4 Cs.

Before you can write good dialogue, you have to know your characters and know them thoroughly: what they think, how they feel, how and where they grew up. They must be three-dimensional people in your mind. As discussed in Chapter Three, simply saying a character is a "waitress" or "cop" isn't nearly enough. Dialogue is often where the rubber meets the road in terms of how well you know your characters. When you know them well, the dialogue feels specific to that individual human being. It feels real, alive. When you don't know your characters, or only know them superficially, the dialogue more likely than not will be bland, generic and clichéd.

As you sit at the keyboard and imagine how the scene you described in your outline will unfold on the imaginary movie screen hovering in front of you, your characters will more than likely begin to speak. Your brain will imagine what they might say. If the character you are writing for is intimately familiar to you — based on someone you know or a combination of people you know or have observed in real life — then this dialogue stands a good chance of being well-written. It is grounded in reality and authentic human speech — in other words, it's in **character**. If, however, you are simply winging it, writing about a character you don't really know or simply basing this character's speech patterns on similar characters you've seen in movies or on TV, then chances are the dialogue won't be as good.

For instance, let's say you are writing the scene described in your outline as "Professor Brown delivers a lecture on morality and ethics to his class." If you've actually taken a philosophy class, you can base this dialogue on the type of things your professor used to say. If, however, you haven't ever taken a philosophy class, do not assume that you can simply guess what you think a philosophy prof sounds like. You need to do some research if you want the dialogue to sound authentic. You might drive over to a local college and sit in on an actual philosophy class. Or you could just stay at your computer, switch from your word processing program over to your Internet access and see if you can find some articles written by philosophy profs on the topic of morality. Or maybe you'll go to YouTube or iTunes, and see if you can find some audio or video podcasts from college profs on morality. You don't need to quote these verbatim (and probably shouldn't), but the point is you'll have a much better chance of capturing the rhythm and professional lingo of a philosophy professor by observing the real thing than by simply pretending you know what these guys sound like. You might also look for quotes from famous philosophers on morality or ethics that the professor could cite.

The same process holds regardless of whether you are writing a football player, a stripper, a homeless person or whomever. You need to capture the sound, vocabulary and cadence of a real human being. To accomplish this, you must either know people like your characters or do some research to gain that sort of knowledge and familiarity. (And to those of you who now feel you must head down to the nearest strip club as a homework assignment, you're welcome.)

Though I've called this research, it's really just one aspect of a larger, more important fundamental of good dialogue: all dialogue must be in **character**. That's the first and most important of the 4 Cs.

For dialogue to be in character — authentic, truthful, believable — you must consider a variety of questions about that character:

- How does this character speak? Formally or informally? Does she swear like a sailor or is she prim and reserved enough to say H-E-double-hockey-sticks rather than use the actual word?
- Who is this character both professionally and personally? Is he a highly educated college philosophy professor who quotes Shakespeare and Greek scholars, or is he a high school drop-out who has lived most of his life on the streets?
- What does the character want at this particular moment in the story?
- Even more important, how does he plan to go about getting what he wants at this moment? Flattery? Deceit? Bullying?

The second of the 4 Cs — **concise** — reflects the difference between conversation (the way people talk in real life) and dialogue (the way characters talk in a movie). Even though, as stressed above, you want your dialogue to be authentic and believable, you don't want it to be real in a literal sense. Real-life conversations ramble; they include unnecessary repetition, irrelevant asides and mistakes. Real-life conversations are rarely as precise as you want screen dialogue to be. In real life, people often take five minutes or five hours to express themselves. Dialogue must capture the essence of what a character wants to express and find a way to convey that essence compactly and, if possible, memorably.

Here is one of my favorite examples of effective, concise dialogue from the feature film *Escape From Alcatraz*, starring Clint Eastwood. Eastwood plays a prisoner at this legendary maximum security lockup. The scene is set in the prison exercise yard. Another prisoner introduces himself to Eastwood and rambles on and on about his personal history, particularly his childhood. On and on and on he goes, with Eastwood simply staring at him. At the end he asks Eastwood, "What kind of childhood did you have?" Eastwood's response, accompanied by his trademark steely glare: "Short."

That's great dialogue. It expresses so much with just one word, because that one word, in the context of the scene, conveys so much subtext. First, of course, it conveys a literal truth: the Eastwood character had a short and probably difficult childhood. But other meanings and implications it captures include *and don't expect me to tell you the details, I don't talk about myself or reveal much,* and *get out of my face, you're bothering me.*

Certainly not every line of dialogue can or should be that brief. In the case of the speech that precedes it — where the other prisoner goes on and on about his upbringing — wordiness is actually the goal. But in general, good dialogue should be as compact as possible.

The two remaining Cs are more or less intuitive, but still merit mention. In addition to being in character and concise, good dialogue is also **connective** and **clear.** By connective I mean that each line of dialogue should be a response to the dialogue or action that immediately precedes it — not necessarily a literal response, but a response motivated by the previous line, including changing the subject entirely if the previous line somehow makes the character uncomfortable. (The exception, of course, is if you are trying to make a point about someone not listening or paying attention to others around him.) Clear means the audience should be able to easily understand the meaning of each line of dialogue. This does not mean that dialogue should always be explicit or "on the nose." Quite the opposite. When dialogue is too "on the nose" it sounds clunky and stilted. Nothing is worse than a character saying something like, "Well here we are, little brother, back in the tiny town of three thousand people where we grew up until Dad left us and Mom tragically committed suicide on Christmas." On the nose, expository dialogue like that is the hallmark of an amateur. A professional would probably handle it by visually showing the arrival of the characters (in a car or on a train) and that we are in a small town. The characters need only say something like, "Feels weird to be back, doesn't it?" Even that is a bit too on the nose. Better still would be a shot of our characters arriving in town, followed by a shot of what they see: a man about their age opening up Watson's Diner, followed by dialogue like, "I guess Opie Watson finally took over the joint from the old man." Though that dialogue doesn't tell us anything about our character's parents, it does give us a clear sense that they used to live here and have been away for a long time. The rest of the information can come out in later dialogue.

Making Your Script Read Visually

As the saying goes, action speaks louder than words — not just in real life, but in film. As cool as it is to write nifty dialogue, films (even short-form Internet episodes) are a visual medium, and the visual is, in most cases, the more powerful, memorable and effective way to connect with the audience. You've no doubt heard this before, but it is Commandment Number One of screenwriting and merits bold print and capital letters: **SHOW DON'T TELL**. Wherever and whenever you can, SHOW us character. Dialogue will no doubt add dimension to your character, but always SHOW us who your characters are through what they do. DRAMATIZE them for us by having their actions and choices ILLUSTRATE and ILLUMINATE who they are deep inside.

Consider the feature film *When Harry Met Sally*. Written by Nora Ephron, the film has some of the sharpest, wittiest dialogue this side of Noël Coward. But if I asked 100 people what they remember most about the film, 98 of them would say "the fake orgasm in the deli scene." In the scene, Sally, played by Meg Ryan, tells Harry it's disgusting that he beds women he barely knows then concocts excuses to flee their bedrooms and run back home as fast as he can. Harry, played by Billy Crystal, defends himself, saying "I think they have a pretty good time" — implying the women are sexually satisfied. Sally asks how he knows they're really satisfied — implying they might be faking their orgasms. Harry, cocky, insists he knows the difference. The dialogue between them is fast, spot-on, highly amusing — and utterly overpowered by what happens next. Sally, in the middle of a crowded New York deli, moans, groans, screams, pounds the table and pretends to have the world's loudest, longest, most mind-blowing orgasm — then calmly sighs, smiles and munches her coleslaw.

The dialogue that precedes it — and a great deal of the dialogue throughout the movie — is top drawer. But actions are always more memorable than even the best dialogue. Seeing Sally demonstrate how easy it is to fake an orgasm is ten times as powerful as any dialogue she can muster to argue that case.

Another tool to help your script read visually is employing active, vivid, descriptive verbs. Beginners often use bland, neutral verbs, like this:

> *Edward enters through the front door. He is tired. He sits on the couch.*

A stronger version of this would be:

> *Edward trudges through the front door, flops on the couch, exhausted.*

Why is the second version better? Because *trudges* paints a stronger visual picture in the reader's mind than *enters*; same goes for *flops* compared to *sits*. As my eighth grade English teacher used to say, verbs are the action words. So use them to help your reader see precisely the type of action you have in mind.

Another common mistake made by novice writers is that they overburden their scripts with an endless litany of unnecessary descriptive detail. *Aren't details good?* you might ask. And my answer would be *yes — but only the important ones.* Students new to screenwriting often set their scenes like this:

```
INT. DAVE'S BEDROOM — DAY

The early morning light shines through half-open
blue Pottery Barn type curtains. DAVE, a thirty-
six-year-old man with curly brown hair and brown
eyes, is asleep in his bed. Clothes hang out of
the open drawers of his IKEA blond wood dresser.
There are also piles of dirty clothes on the
floor — some jeans, T-shirts, a grey suit, socks
and underwear, plus Dave's beloved hockey skates
and goalie pads. There is a clock radio on the
nightstand, along with an empty bottle of Jose
Cuervo Especial Gold 80 and some mostly-eaten
slices of pepperoni, mushroom and onion pizza.
```

> The clock radio flips over from 5:59 to 6:00
> and U2's "Mysterious Ways" begins to play. Dave
> groans, reaches over and turns off the clock
> radio. He sits up, gets out of bed, and walks
> into the bathroom.

I'll spare you the even lengthier description of the bathroom that typically follows. But rest assured that it is similarly flooded by a tsunami of irrelevant details. The job of the screenwriter is to direct the reader's eye to those details that are absolutely essential and most revealing. Who cares what color the curtains are, which items of clothing are on the floor, or what kind of pizza Dave likes? Does it matter what color his eyes are, or that his hair is curly? NO. Here's a better way to handle this scene:

INT. DAVE'S BEDROOM – EARLY MORNING

DAVE (36) snores in the middle of a frat-boy mess of dirty clothes and discarded pizza boxes. Suddenly, the clock radio BLARES U2. Dave groans, knocks over what's left of a bottle of tequila as he slaps at the clock, then stumbles out of bed and trips over some hockey gear on the way to the bathroom.

In less than half the words we still get the complete picture — in fact, an improved picture because now the important details, uncluttered by the trivial ones, stand out. Furthermore, the images resemble a moving picture rather than a static one because they are revealed through action. The pig-sty environment is revealed as Dave snores (snoring being a more active picture than "is asleep"). The previous night's tequila is revealed not as a "still photo" or snapshot, but as a moving image, knocked over when Dave reaches for the clock. Same thing for the hockey gear — it is revealed through action, when Dave trips over it.

In short, use every language tool at your disposal to make your script read like a movie rather than a short story.

You've Got A First Draft — Time To Get To Work Again

First drafts are exactly that: a good beginning. Pat yourself on the back for a job well done. Celebrate with your favorite age-appropriate beverage. Smile at yourself in the mirror and give yourself a well-deserved finger gun. You did it! You da (insert gender)!

Okay, celebration over. Now it's time to wipe that smug grin off your face and get back to work. *But you just said I did it! I'm the man/woman/other*! And you are — you're totally awesome. But a first draft is far from a polished final script. You must now take your first draft, read it with a cold, objective eye, assess its strengths and weaknesses. You must read it as if someone else had written it and you were being asked for your honest, no-holds-barred opinion of each and every word.

Your Inner Creator has accomplished something miraculous: he has delivered a real script, a story with dialogue and action in screenplay form that can serve as a blueprint for a short-form Internet pilot. Bravo! But now your Inner Creator must take a step back and let his trusted and valued partner, your Inner Editor, do his work too. The Inner Editor's work begins with "big picture" questions as he reads:

- Is the premise of the series clearly defined based on what is shown in this one script?
- Can you imagine other stories based on this premise — a lot of other stories?
- Is it clear who the main character is?
- Is it clear what the main character wants and what prevents him from getting what he wants? Can it be made more clear, or presented in a more palpable or memorable way?
- Are each of the characters clearly defined through their action and dialogue? Are there any places, large or small, where the characters can be more sharply defined?
- Does each scene advance the story?
- Are there people out there who will be interested in this story and these characters?

Your reflexive answer to each of these questions will be *Of course all these things are clear and as good as they can be. I wrote it and it's perfect.* Trust me, it's not perfect. Nobody — not Emmy-winning, Hall of Fame (if there were such a thing) TV writers, not even William Shakespeare himself, ever wrote a first draft that didn't need rewriting. You must discipline yourself to avoid the natural, defensive tendency to 1) deflect all criticism, even if it comes from you; and 2) just want to be done with the damn thing and move on and shoot the sucker.

The key, I think, is looking at the "criticism" your Inner Editor is dishing out not as a personal attack, but more like the way you might feel when your significant other informs you, just as you're about to leave the house, that the seam in your jeans has split and you really should change unless you want people to see all the way to Adventureland when you sit down. You'd thank them for pointing this out, wouldn't you?

When I get valid criticism of my first drafts — whether it comes from me or from someone else — I'm grateful that I've been saved from exposing my less than best effort to the world. Sure, my first reaction to the criticism is *F*&k you, you're an idiot and I hate you and your children are ugly.* But experience has taught me to set that defensive, unproductive reaction aside and consider the note being given. Can I improve my characters, or my dialogue? Is there a better way to dramatize that point?

If you can approach rewriting not as a chore, but as an opportunity to take something good and make it better, not only will your scripts improve, but you'll find the process of rewriting much more enjoyable.

In addition to the list of "big picture" questions, you will also want to examine things on a microscopic, word by word level:

- Is every verb in my description and action lines as vivid and active as possible?
- Is each line of dialogue in character? Would this character say "eat dinner" or would he say "dine" or "grab a bite" or "chow down"?
- Is each speech and line of description as concise as possible?

When Is It Ready To Be Shot?

Obviously, I'm big on not shooting your first draft. You must rewrite your script, and probably rewrite it several times. But sooner or later you'll need to ask the question *How do I know when I'm done?*

It's a fair question. No script is ever perfect, but neither are you writing the script simply to archive your pages. You are writing it because you want to shoot it, edit it, and post it on the Web for people to see — which can't happen if you are eternally stuck in an endless loop of writing and rewriting. So the question isn't when is your script perfect, but when is it ready to be shot?

Unfortunately, there is no software currently available that can analyze your script and pronounce it worthy of production or not. But if you have gone through the process of developing your pilot concept and characters, writing an outline for your pilot story, writing a first draft, reading and honestly assessing that first draft, rewriting to improve it, then rereading and rewriting those improved drafts several times, then I think you are ready to shoot — or at least have a script that is ready to shoot. Preparing for the actual shoot — also known as preproduction, is the subject of our next chapter.

● FOR TEACHERS…

The best way to help students grasp the strengths and weaknesses of their scripts — especially their first drafts — is to have them read aloud in class. Assign the parts, including someone other than the writer to read the action descriptions, and give your students the chance to hear their work performed just as it might be in a professional setting at a table reading.

Hearing a script read aloud quickly exposes poorly written dialogue, excessively overwritten description, and other common rookie screenwriting mistakes. It also highlights the places where your students have written good dialogue and effective, economical description. Either way, the quality of the work or lack thereof becomes more palpably apparent when scripts are read aloud than when they are read silently.

One issue teachers must always confront at this stage is finding the line between guiding the student and doing the rewrite for them. Some Socratic academic purists insist that the instructor must never "give the student the answer" and therefore refuse to offer concrete suggestions for how to improve dialogue, description, character or structural elements. I find this approach needlessly pedantic. Certainly I won't rewrite a whole scene or even a whole page for a student. But if I feel their dialogue needs work, for instance, I try to offer two or three examples of improved versions of their lines.

One other point worth making to the students about reading scripts aloud: learning opportunities abound not just when your own script is read, but in listening carefully and thoughtfully when analyzing your classmates' scripts. A big part of growing as a writer is learning how to dissect and analyze screenplays in progress, whether they are your own or the work of a colleague. Students should be encouraged to offer critiques and analyses of each other's work — a valuable skill not only to improve their own writing, but as basic training for entering the professional world, where the ability to discuss and analyze scripts and pitches is a fundamental part of the job description. So remind your students that they are to be mentally engaged at all times — whether the script being discussed is their own or someone else's. Even better, call on them when discussing their classmates' work. Force them to voice an opinion.

CHAPTER SEVEN

CHOOSING A VISUAL STYLE

The late Brandon Tartikoff, the renowned former president of NBC and self-described TV addict, was so obsessed with MTV and the revolution it brought to visual storytelling in the early 1980s that legend has it he scribbled "MTV Cops" on a scrap of paper, handed it to a writer/producer and said "that's the show I want." The show he got, based on that two-word scrawl, was the breakthrough series *Miami Vice*. Though the show had excellent stories and characters, its greatest impact on TV was its visual style and the way it revolutionized the use of modern "MTV techniques" in telling visual stories on television in the modern era. These techniques included faster-paced editing, non-linear imagery and juxtaposition, and the liberal use of current popular music as a soundtrack. Tartikoff understood that television is a visual medium and that visual style is just as important to the appeal and success of shows in the post-MTV era as story, character, premise, or any other content element.

All good TV shows, including shows designed for distribution on the Web, have a specific and thoughtfully designed visual style. Consider the network TV series *24* and *The Office*. Each has a distinctive visual presentation that is not only eye-catching, but supports and enhances the underlying content and themes. The "spy cam" shots and direct address to the camera by the actors in *The Office* reinforce the connection between the audience and the show. They emphasize the sense that we, the audience, are merely eavesdropping on real conversations in an actual office just like the ones we all work in. The intimacy of the style — actors addressing the audience directly and the almost "home video" feel to some of the camerawork — intensifies the audience's sense that they are not only observing the action, but are "insiders" or participants of a sort themselves. In other words, the visual presentation of the show enhances the "audience bond".

In the case of *24*, the split screens and superimposed ticking digital clock constantly remind us that our hero, Jack Bauer, has too many problems to juggle and not nearly enough time. The visual elements of *24* are not merely eye candy, they are also vital elements that crank up the underlying tension that propels the show and the story it is telling. Jack Bauer is fighting against "a ticking time bomb" and the on-screen graphics constantly remind us of that intense pressure.

In the Internet-TV realm, take a look at shows like *Web Therapy* and *We Need Girlfriends*. Much of *Web Therapy* is shot "webcam" style, reminding us that this is 3-minute Internet therapy, not traditional doctor's-office/50-minute-hour therapy. It also reinforces, much like the spy cam in *The Office*, the sense that we are somehow privy to confidential conversations, seeing things that were meant to be private but have somehow magically been captured for our enjoyment. And the "amateur" feel of the webcam angles — as opposed to a finely crafted and framed feature film-style composition — reinforces the sense that Fiona (played by Lisa Kudrow) is a less than professional practitioner of therapy.

We Need Girlfriends incorporates shaky handheld camera, visually emphasizing the sense that these less-than-mature, slacker slobs have fairly shaky lives.

While much of the visual distinction of these shows is executed during production and postproduction, it begins with the script. Your pilot script should convey, either explicitly or implicitly, not just what the show is about, but what it should look like. This does not — repeat, in capital letters, DOES NOT — mean you should attempt to "direct" the script on the page. You would NOT want to write a scene for *Web Therapy* like this:

```
INT. FIONA'S OFFICE — DAY

Fiona conducts a "web therapy" session with a
client. The CAMERA, with a wide-angle, 14mm lens,
is placed low, as if on her desk.
```

As soon as you begin talking about cameras and lenses, the reader stops visualizing a scene unfolding on his mental movie screen and begins seeing a film shoot, complete with lights and cameras and a grip drinking coffee in a Styrofoam cup while he scratches his hairy butt crack with a hammer. This takes the reader out of the movie, breaks the spell, the magical, dreamlike continuity of a story being told, and instead connects them with the nuts and bolts and sweat and tedium of filmmaking. While you want to convey a sense of the visual, you want to keep your reader connected to what he sees on the screen, not how it is accomplished. A better approach would be this:

```
INT. FIONA'S OFFICE — DAY

Fiona conducts a "web therapy" session with
a client, speaking directly into the webcam
embedded in the laptop on her desk.
```

The Marriage Of Style And Content

As outlined in the above discussion, visual style is not something random, something welded onto your show merely because it "looks cool." The visual style you choose and develop for your series should be inextricably intertwined with the content, theme and world of your story and characters.

Is your show quiet and intimate? If so, the visuals should reflect this — not just in choice of camera angles and the pace of editing, but in the production design and choice of locations. Intimacy implies private settings, close-ups, shots of small details that reveal the inner thoughts and feelings of the characters. Your script should reflect these "intimate" choices, which will then be augmented, enhanced and emphasized by the camera choices during production.

Or maybe your script is about a stressed-out mom trying to juggle kids, a career and a marriage or dating life. In that case, you'll want the writing to embody the overloaded, multitasking nature of your main character's life. Maybe you'll want to borrow from 24, and use split screens showing her negotiating a deal on her cell phone while she bathes her infant on one screen, talking to her six-year-old on the phone while her lover undresses her on another, eating and writing a memo on a third screen, and writing a grocery list while she pees on a fourth screen. Short, quick scenes might also be called for, and frenetic montage.

There are infinite variations and infinite choices — but the one choice you should not make is to ignore the visual. You are writing not just for the page, but for the screen. Content without style or style without content are equally unacceptable. You must have both, and they should be inextricably interwoven.

Beginnings, Endings And Transitions

One of the most effective ways to give your series a distinctive visual and/or aural signature is through the parts of the show that bind it together — the main title, the end credits, and the transitions between scenes. Think of the main title for 24 — the number 24, in digital readout typeface, jumping closer and closer to you, each jump reinforced by the loud, echoing "countdown" sound, as if a bomb were about to explode. You're tense already, right? Or consider the opening title of *The Guild* and its light-hearted animation and upbeat but ironic music. It sends the message that this show, in part, is about people who participate in a fantasy world, and that this is a comedy, not a drama.

Transitions — how your series moves from scene to scene — can also enhance the visual signature and identity of your show. *Law & Order* is a classic example of how important and valuable transitions can be. I'd venture to say that if you mentioned that classic TV series to most viewers, the first two things about the show that would spring to mind are 1) the music from the main title; and 2) the *dun-dun* sound effect they use to transition from one scene to the next. That sound effect, simple as it is, adds a great deal to the show. Coupled with the usual on-screen printout setting time and place, it conveys a sense of drama, of realism, and of the gritty world of law enforcement. And it does this in less than two seconds, and is so memorable that it can legitimately be considered an invaluable part of the show's brand identity.

The CBS comedy *The Big Bang Theory* also has wonderful transitions — animated sequences of planetary activity or sub-atomic collisions. They are both intellectual and offbeat at once — just like the characters in the series.

Finally, we come to the end credits. All shows have them — either because they employ high-budget, union cast and crew and are contractually bound to include the names on screen, or because they are low-budget or no-budget productions and giving credit to those who worked so hard to make the show is the least they could do to thank them. In either case, just rolling a list of the names of staff and crew against a black background in silence is not only boring, it is a wasted opportunity. If you are doing a comedy, make your end credits comedic. Network sitcoms commonly use a short comedic scene or "tag" as the background for the end credit sequence. Or they might use outtakes — humorous mistakes and screw-ups recorded during production — as the background. The feature film *Airplane!* literally embedded jokes in the endless text of the end title crawl. The chief assistant to the key grip or lighting gaffer on a film is known as the best boy. So Jerry Zucker, David Zucker and Jim Abrahams included the following in their end credit crawl:

Best Boy..........Joe Schmo
Worst Boy..........Adolph Hitler

They also spiced up the litany of credits for makeup artists, visual effects supervisors and the like with occasional credits like:

Thirteenth President of the United States..........Millard Fillmore

Or this:

Foreez..........The Jolly Good Fellow

They even found a way to get humor out of the densely worded legalese about copyright law at the end, like this:

This Motion Picture Is Protected Under The Laws Of The United States And Other Countries. Unauthorized Duplication, Distribution, Or Exhibition May Result In Civil Liability And Criminal Prosecution, So There.

So don't ignore things like credit sequences and transitions. Nothing should be taken for granted. Every second of your show, every frame, is a creative opportunity. The more the obligatory (credits) can contribute to the content, tone and branding of your series, the better.

● FOR TEACHERS...

As this chapter indicates, visual considerations are not an afterthought, and should not be segregated from the script process or reserved for production only. Talk to your students about the importance of the visual while they are developing their scripts. Screen examples for them of effective main titles, transitions and end credit sequences. If possible, show them script excerpts that demonstrate how the visual style of that show was conceived long before a frame of footage was ever shot — right there on the page.

Also be sure to make clear to them the difference between writing visually (a good thing) and obsessively trying to direct the film on paper, which makes the script thoroughly tedious, breaks the spell of the story, and ultimately makes the script unreadable.

CHAPTER EIGHT
PRACTICAL CONCERNS — EQUIPMENT AND BUDGET

How much does it cost to make a pilot or an episode of an *Internet TV series?* That, as the Greatest Generation used to say, is the $64,000 Question — a reference to the name of a popular TV quiz show of the 1950s. Of course, the show began on the radio, during the Depression Generation, where it was simply called *The $64 Question*. So, as you might surmise, the answer to the question *How much does it cost to make an Internet TV series?* is yet another question — in fact, a series of questions:

> *How much money do you have?*
> *What are the production requirements of your script?*
> *What resources do you already have?*
> *What resources can you beg, borrow or steal?*
> *How creative can you be?*

How you answer these questions will determine your budget. The creators of *Sanctuary* had a script that called for elaborate special effects and aspirations to deliver a top-notch science fiction epic of feature film length. They also had extensive credits in the business and were, therefore, able to obtain financing for their $4.2-million budget. At the other end of the financial scale, Rob McElhenney, Glenn Howerton and Charlie Day, the creators of *It's Always Sunny In Philadelphia*, managed to shoot its half-hour pilot for $75 — the cost of the videotape. How were they able to shoot a pilot good enough to attract a major cable network series order on so little money? Through their creativity in using the resources they already had or could get their hands on for nothing. They wrote a script that could be shot in locations they could obtain access to for free, that they could act in themselves, wearing their own clothes, using props they already had lying around, and which could be shot without needing lights or any equipment beyond a simple camcorder which they already owned (or perhaps borrowed).

The show is now in its fourth season on FX and is considered a landmark comedy.

Albert Einstein famously said "Imagination is more important than knowledge." I'd add to that by saying imagination is also more important than money.

If you've got access to financing or have a rich uncle or a nest egg of your own you're willing to tap into, then by all means feel free to use your imagination to create whatever big-budget extravaganza your heart desires to see on the screen. If, however, you're like most people — long on dreams but short on cash — then get creative. Use your imagination to come up with a premise that can be produced with whatever resources and cash you can scrape together.

Equipment: From The Bargain Basement To The Penthouse

Whether you make movies, enjoy fishing or golf, or spend your weekends wailing away on a vintage electric guitar as part of an aging boomer garage band called The Not So Grateful Nearly Dead, there's nothing more mesmerizing than dreaming about just how great you could be if only you could buy that primo, top-of-the-line equipment. We all want bigger, better, fancier, more expensive toys, partly because shopping is fun, and partly because we all labor under the delusion that we're natural-born superstars just waiting to be discovered — if only we had the money to buy that great new (fill in the blank: Titanium Tiger Woods model driver, Eric Clapton signature guitar, or Red One camera). The people who manufacture and market all this high-end gear spend millions of dollars on advertising and marketing in order to perpetuate this grand delusion. It's how they make money, selling you far more than you need or could ever make good use of.

So let's get real. When it comes right down to it, what equipment do you absolutely, positively, really need in order to write, shoot, edit and upload your short-form TV series to the Internet? Here's the list:

A computer. Doesn't have to be the Steve Jobs signature model Mac TurboPro 5000 LX Titanium Edition (if there was such a thing). But you will need a basic computer of some sort, with Internet access, preferably broadband, not dial-up. Chances are your computer will include another necessary component: **editing software**, which gives you the ability to edit the video you shoot into the most effective sequence of shots. Right now, I'm typing this sentence on a lower-priced, four-year-old Dell laptop. Even though I didn't specifically request it, it came with Windows Movie Maker, common editing software, installed automatically along with Spider Solitaire. If you own a PC, I'll bet you already have this useful editing software yourself, hidden under **Programs>Accessories>Windows Movie Maker**. If you own a Mac, you'll have iMovies or something similar.

A video camera. Your basic home model will do just fine for most projects and concepts. Your camera will almost certainly include the ability to record **sound**, including a built-in microphone.

That's it, the whole shebang.

Really?

Really. Just ask the guys who made *It's Always Sunny In Philadelphia*.

You won't be able to make something that looks or sounds like *Star Wars*, or even like an episode of *CSI*. But you will be able to make something as entertaining, engaging and appealing as your imagination can conjure.

That said, let's be honest. If all you have is a basic camcorder, there will be limitations you must take into consideration. If you don't have a tripod, your video will look shaky and handheld — because it will be. The sound you record from the microphone that comes mounted on the camera will be distant and hollow in most situations. Shooting at night or in dark interiors may be difficult or impossible.

In short, your series stands a good chance of having the look and feel of amateur home video. This may be exactly what you want — say, if you've created a series that is a video diary of a stoner college student, or a heavy metal band on tour. But if your premise demands a more "polished" or professional feel to what you see and hear, you may need to invest some money in obtaining slightly more than the rock bottom basics.

So for those of you with higher production value goals, and for those of you who, like me, crave more and better toys (my weakness is fancy acoustic guitars), here's the lowdown on more sophisticated, more powerful, and more expensive equipment you may want to know about.

Cameras And Camera Accessories

As I mentioned above, one piece of inexpensive equipment that can instantly elevate your camerawork from shaky amateur to steady and sure filmmaker is a **tripod**. They run anywhere from about $20 for a bare-bones model to several hundred dollars for something professional. To learn more about tripods (and almost every other aspect of video equipment and filmmaking technique), go to *mediacollege.com*.

If you don't already own a video camera, the choices nowadays are nearly infinite. A search of the Internet site CNET Reviews under "digital video cameras" presently yields a list of 188 under $200, 34 over $2,700 (all the way up to $23,625 for the Panasonic AJ HDX900 professional), and nearly 300 other choices in between. A fully-loaded high-end HD camera with lenses and accessories can easily run more than $100,000. But the question isn't *what's the best camera?* but rather *what's the best camera for you and your project and what do you really need?*

My students at Chapman University have access to a range of video cameras, from basic all the way up to high-definition Varicams capable of capturing image quality and detail worthy of a big-budget extravaganza at your local multiplex. In the classes I teach on Byte-Sized Television, where they make original web series, when I ask them which camera they want to use, they almost always shout out excitedly, "The Varicam!" But when I ask them *why* they want to use the Varicam, their answers basically boil down to, "Because it's cool." Then I remind them that the audience they're hoping to reach with their series will probably be watching on a laptop computer, with, at most, a 17-inch screen. I also remind them that the HD tape cassettes for the Varicam cost about $130 each and could easily eat up more than half of their per-episode budget. The standard definition cameras, however, use mini-DV cassettes which are so inexpensive that the school provides them for free. I usually finish my pitch for the "lesser" cameras by screening some of the best work done the previous year using those "lesser" cameras. The inevitable response from my students is, "That looks pretty darn good."

Another point worth making is that you don't have to buy every single piece of equipment — you can rent. Over the long haul, if you continue to make dozens of episodes, you'll certainly want to own the basic elements you use over and over again, like your camera and tripod. But it may also make a great deal of sense to rent what you need the first few times out, evaluate whether each piece of equipment serves your needs, and how often, and then make a decision about whether to buy it or rent it only when needed.

Sound — Mikes, Booms, Recorders, Etc.

Sound and how it will be recorded is commonly the last thing non-professionals give any thought to when setting out to make a short video. Sound is, unfortunately and unfairly, pretty much taken for granted, unnoticed and underappreciated by audiences — right up until the sound is bad, at which time they complain bitterly. Sound quality is also the very first thing that separates a well-made and engaging web series from — to use a highly technical term — an unwatchable pile of dog crap.

Think back to the home videos your dad shot of you when you were little and he was all geeked about buying his first video camera. You were putting on your Little League uniform, or your ballet tutu, or maybe just minding your own business in your room. Dad was about ten feet away, standing in the doorway, pointing this alien-looking camera thing with a little red light at you. The scene and dialogue no doubt went something like this:

INT. BEDROOM — DAY

BRANDON "HOME RUN" STERNE (9), wearing a Little League Uniform that says "Giants" on the front and "State Farm Insurance" on the back, double-knots the laces on his rubber cleats. He is happily daydreaming of circling the bases in a victorious home run trot when his reverie is broken by an imposing shadow, the smell of his father's Polo cologne, and an annoying mechanical whirring noise. Brandon turns, sees his father DOUG pointing the new video camera at him.

>   DOUG
>   (a little too loud, a little
>   too cheery)
>   Hey, bud. Whatcha up to?

Brandon mumbles something unintelligible into his chest.

                    DOUG
             (even louder)
        What? I couldn't hear you.

Brandon makes a vague attempt to mumble louder.
He either says "smoking," "hiking" or "nothing"
— impossible to tell because Doug's hollow
breathing is right on top of the microphone
built into the camera, overpowering any other
sound in the room. Doug walks two steps closer
and squats down closer to Brandon.

                    DOUG
        Say it again.

                    BRANDON
             (screams into camera)
        NOTHING!!!

You get the idea — a home video classic, probably hauled out
for public viewing every other Christmas or so. The audio inevitably sounds like it was recorded inside the trunk of a rusty old
Chevy. Though camcorders have come a long way since Madonna
sang about being like a virgin, and the built-in mikes are far more
capable, there's no avoiding the trademark hollowness of sound
recorded by a microphone that is closer to the camera and its
operator than to the person speaking. If that's the look and feel
you're going for in your series, by all means use that distinctive
sound quality to your advantage. I'm serious. Let's say you've
created a web series entitled *My Parents Are F***ED UP!* The
premise is a teenager interviews his parents, secretly films them
when they aren't aware, and then comments on all of it. It would
be absolutely WRONG in my opinion to record the sound of the
parents speaking using a separate microphone on a boom. The
premise and picture demand the hollow, distant sound quality of
a home video camera, and the best, fastest, easiest way to create
that is (duh!) by recording the sound using the built-in mike
attached to the camera. In this scenario, the filmmaker clearly
WANTS to call attention to the filmmaking process. He WANTS
the audience to be aware of the camera, and of the microphone,

and of the fact that this is being recorded mockumentary style. It's the perfect situation for turning a disadvantage (no money to rent professional equipment and no crew to work with that equipment) into a stylistic advantage and signature technique of your project.

If, however, you've got a different sort of premise, one where you just want the story to unfold on screen in a traditional fashion — seamlessly, realistically, without making the audience aware of the equipment and crew — then you'll need to use some of the tools that the pros use to accomplish this. You'll want the camera to be steady (see above section on benefits of a tripod) and you'll want the sound to be crisp, clean and even, the way it is in a movie or scripted TV show.

In order to achieve this, you'll need to record the sound using a microphone that can be placed the appropriate distance from the person speaking. This, in turn, may also mean you'll need a "boom" — an extendable pole with the mike attached to the end of it that can be held above the actors' heads, out of the picture frame, to record the sound from the best possible angle for emphasizing what is being said and de-emphasizing extraneous background noises. If you employ a boom, clearly you'll need some crew other than yourself. If you are operating the camera, you'll need someone to hold the boom pole and point the microphone at the actor or actors who are speaking.

Depending on the scene and its requirements, other types of microphones may be needed. For instance if your scene calls for two people jogging and talking, having a boom operator running alongside them with a pole above his head isn't very practical. In that case, you may choose to employ wireless mikes.

As with camera technique, the complete ins and outs of recording production sound are far more complex than can be covered in a few pages. Entire books have been written about the subject. If your webisodes only require the basics, then this brief discussion may be enough. But if you need more detail, consult the list of books and resources in Appendix 2 and get the information that will help you.

Lights

If your script calls for filming in a space without enough available light to allow the audience to see the details you want them to see (e.g., the actor's eyes, or printed words on a note or book), then you will need to use lights. They don't have to be fancy, studio-quality lights. Ordinary household lamps can often work just fine. Michael Buckley lights the simple set of his Internet celebrity dish-fest *What The Buck* using a pair of work lights from Home Depot. As of December 2008 the show had accumulated more than 100 million hits on YouTube — and to my knowledge, not a single person has commented on the lighting as yet.

The key questions are what do you want your images to look like on screen, and how can you accomplish that? If you are shooting an interrogation scene and want the effect of a super-bright light being blasted into the suspect's face, then you'll need to find a light with enough firepower to achieve that effect — one ever so much brighter than the rest of the light sources.

By far the most difficult environment in which to mold the lighting into the look you want is the night exterior. Furthermore, the larger the area you want to photograph outside at night, the more lights you will likely need. And each of those lights will need a power source which, in turn, may mean you'll need a generator to provide that power. So unless you have easy access to lights and power, or unless you have a substantial budget to work with, you might want to rewrite that panoramic night exterior scene and reset it in an easier location to film — an interior, or a park bench or other small, controllable, easily lit exterior.

Editing Software — Fancier Stuff

No area of filmmaking has benefited more from the digital revolution than editing and postproduction. A veritable smorgasbord of software is available that allows you to upload video to your computer, edit it swiftly and efficiently in a nonlinear manner, and to add titles, transitions, sound effects and narration. Even better news is the fact that a great deal of this software is inexpensive or free, installed at no charge on your computer when you bought it.

The basic default editing programs that come with your computer are Windows Movie Maker (for PC) and iMovies (Mac). If you have a little money and want to investigate other choices, *toptenreviews.com* rates CyberLink PowerDirector, Corel VideoStudio and Adobe Premiere Elements as its top video editing software choices for 2009. All are available for under $90.

For those who crave greater editing sophistication and capabilities, Apple's line of Final Cut products is the consensus choice. Available for Mac or PC, they range from the $200 Final Cut Express all the way up to Final Cut Studio, a professional-quality product with nearly infinite editing, sound and graphic tools. It runs about $1,300.

As with the other equipment categories, you don't need to breathlessly rush online to Hardcore Software Junkies 'R' Us and max out your credit card on the biggest, baddest and best software package available. First check out the stuff you've already got on your computer for free. See how it works, if it fits your needs. Then, if you bump up against the ceiling of its capabilities, you'll have a much clearer idea whether you need the $200 upgrade or if you really do want to consider auctioning off your next ovulation on eBay to finance that Final Cut Studio purchase.

Learning More About All This Equipment And How To Use It

For some of us who consider learning how to text message a major technological accomplishment, the thought of learning about digital filmmaking and editing can be overwhelming. To others, navigating the technology is from The Big Book of Duh, but you could use some help knowing how to use it to capture and edit the elements necessary to tell an effective story, or learning about the more subtle and sophisticated tricks of the video trade.

Obviously, the book you hold in your hands right now is a good place to start. But no one book can tell you everything you need to know about making videos from soup to nuts. I have chosen to focus more on the creative process here than on the technical aspects. But the good news is that there are excellent books and instructional resources available that can teach you whatever else you might need to learn. Know lots about video capture but zip about how to frame a shot? Or how to storyboard a scene before you shoot it? Or the principles of editing an action scene? Or how to create the best possible soundtrack? Not a problem. Appendix 2 has a list of books that offer in-depth discussions and instruction on all areas of video and audio craft and technology.

● FOR TEACHERS…

There are many challenges in helping students select and acquire access to the equipment most appropriate and useful to their production. One of the challenges is moderating their natural enthusiasm for "stuff that seems cool," like wanting to shoot in HD when standard definition is really what's called for and affordable, or begging for a dolly or crane because they're still buzzing with excitement from seeing the latest Michael Bay kinetic epic. While I am a big believer in ultimately letting the student make the final decision (within budget and other limitations) about how they want to shoot their video, I also believe it is the role of the instructor to challenge them to justify their choices. If they only have ten hours to shoot on one day, and need to get twenty setups in the can, is it really worth spending the hours it will take to set up a dolly shot for that first master which may only be on screen for five or six seconds?

At the other end of the spectrum, sometimes students don't realize the tools they might have at their disposal. While a dolly might be expensive and time-consuming, if the shot is of two people moving down a hallway talking, then borrowing an office chair and rolling the camera operator down the hall in front of the actors might work just fine, giving the audience a sense of motion while still being able to move quickly and not get bogged down laying and leveling dolly track.

When it comes to expenses and equipment, the teacher's role is to provide limits, but also to provide imagination and creative ways to get the most bang for your inevitably limited production buck.

CHAPTER NINE
THE PILOT –
PREPRODUCTION

"Failure to prepare is preparing to fail."
— John Wooden, Hall of Fame basketball coach

"Every battle is won before it is fought."
— Sun Tzu, *The Art of War*

Coach Wooden and Sun Tzu could just as well have been talking about shooting a pilot. You can't just show up with your camcorder and wing it. You must prepare thoughtfully and thoroughly if you want your production days — and, in turn, your pilot — to be successful.

In a sense, you've been in preproduction all along as you conceptualized your series and characters and developed your script. You've already created a blueprint for what the finished product will look like on screen. The characters you'll need, the settings, the crucial props and wardrobe are all no doubt delineated in your script. But now you must take the next step and turn those words and images in your script into a physical reality that can be captured on video. The characters you dreamed up have to be played by actors. The settings you imagined must become actual locations found in real life, and you'll need to get permission from the owners of these locations. The scenes you created on paper must now be captured shot by shot, and you'll need to plan each of those shots ahead of time, visualize them in your mind before you show up to shoot, because that's the only way to make sure that you have all the tools to execute your vision.

Preproduction requires discipline, attention to each and every detail of your proposed shoot, and the ability to adapt the creative vision you hold in your mind to the physical and financial realities of the world. Just as carefully developing your story and outline were crucial to the eventual success of your script, the time and effort you put into preproduction can make or break your pilot. Sloppy and half-hearted preproduction inevitably leads to a chaotic, frustrating and often disastrous shoot. But careful, thoughtful and thorough preproduction leads to maximum creative freedom and productivity when the camera is rolling and the actors are performing.

So don't take shortcuts. Put your best focused effort into each of the following phases of preproduction.

Casting: Finding Talented Actors When You Have No Budget

Anybody can put together a great cast when they've got a multi-million-dollar budget. You hire a casting director; they put the word out to the major talent agencies that represent all of the best-known actors. Scripts are emailed, phone calls exchanged, lunch is done, the spa cuisine is ordered, and offers are made. If you've got that kind of budget and contacts, my guess is that you don't need this book to tell you how it's done.

But what about the other 99.99999% of the world — those of us not plugged into the Hollywood power elite? How on Earth can we find good actors to perform in our projects when we've barely got enough money to buy bagels and soft drinks for the skeleton crew working for free?

The first logical question is why not act in it yourself, or get your friends to act in your pilot? The answer to that question, however, may be that you and your friends aren't actors. If your premise is reality-based — say a series about your family — then this approach might work. The guys who created *It's Always*

Sunny In Philadelphia did, after all, not only use themselves as the cast for their $75 pilot, but they still continued to appear as the main cast of the show (along with Danny DeVito and Caitlin Olsen) even after they had a substantial budget and a contract with FX. But in many instances, your premise and script will require finding skilled actors who can perform at a professional level but are still willing to work for little or no money.

There are several ways to find experienced and extremely capable actors like this. If you live in or near a major city, there will no doubt be online sites where you can post the specifics of the roles you are looking to cast. Actors will then contact you and you can set up auditions. Examples of this type of site are *nowcasting.com* in Los Angeles and *talentzoo.com* in Atlanta. I found out about the later simply by typing "casting Atlanta" in a Google search box. So do the same for the city near you and see what you find.

Whether or not you live near a major urban center, there is almost certainly a small theater of some kind somewhere near you that puts on plays. They may have a regular company of actors, or they may search for them on a project-by-project basis, just like you're about to do. In either case, contact them, tell them what you're looking for, and see if they can help by either suggesting actors or sharing how they find talent.

As an example of this, early in my career I worked as an assistant director on an extremely low-budget movie. There were half a dozen small parts — maybe half a dozen lines each — which the producer had not cast but expected me to fill. I knew that I couldn't just throw some inexperienced friends out there in front of the camera; these were speaking parts and somehow I needed to find a handful of trained actors willing to work for the budgeted sum of $35 per day. So I contacted this small L.A. improv comedy group called The Groundlings. Though they performed in a hole-in-the-wall space themselves at that time, they had been a launching pad for several actors who later made it big. I told them what I was looking for, what it paid, and they got me half a dozen terrific young performers who did a bang-up job for basically gas money. One of these thirty-five bucks a day actors was the young Phil Hartman, later a major star on *Saturday Night Live*.

A third widely available resource is the theater department at any nearby university or community college. Young actors are by nature eager to work, willing to do so for the experience even if there isn't any money involved, and often bring a phenomenal amount of enthusiasm and creative energy to the work. So contact the theater department, or post a notice on their bulletin board, and see what you can find. Not everyone will be great, but I'd almost bet that you'll find more than a few performers who will absolutely blow you away with how good they are.

Locations: Imagination Meets Reality

When you wrote your script you could no doubt visualize each and every location you described in precise detail, right down to the little dings in the furniture. You could almost smell the suntan lotion glistening on the perfectly tanned legs of those dancers lounging by the pool of the Bellagio Hotel in Vegas, or taste the hot dogs and beer your slacker buddy characters were eating in that scene set at Yankee Stadium.

But now that you are not just writing a script but planning an actual shoot, the unlimited potential of your imagination must contend with the litany of limitations that the real world often presents. There's a good chance you may not be allowed to shoot at the Bellagio or Yankee Stadium. And don't even think about trying to shoot at a place like that without obtaining permission. Often you may be able to get permission to film your dream location, only to discover that the price tag for doing so is prohibitive. These types of obstacles can occur not only with grand locations like fancy hotels or ballparks, but with almost anyplace other than your own house or apartment. Many stores and businesses find film crews disruptive and want no part of being in a film or TV show. Even open public spaces, like parks, may restrict your ability to shoot that location or may require you to obtain expensive permits and hire park personnel for the day to "supervise" your activity.

If you encounter these roadblocks, does it mean you should just chuck your concept, burn the script and start over again? Absolutely not. But it may mean you need to get creative and make some adjustments. Maybe your Vegas dancers aren't lounging by the Bellagio pool but rather are gathered around the ordinary pool at one of their modest apartment buildings — because you live in an apartment building in Arizona that looks just like that. Or maybe your slackers aren't talking during the game but on the way to the game — because you *can* get permission to shoot *on the street near Yankee Stadium* and it looks great in the background.

Another creative approach to overcoming location hurdles is imitating a location rather than shooting at the real thing. For instance, you might be able to shoot an establishing shot of the Bellagio (with a camcorder out front just like a tourist), then film two dancers on lounge chairs at some other pool, but keep the shots tight enough that all we see is dancers in lounge chairs with blue water behind them. The audience will *think* it's the Bellagio because of the establishing shot, even though the dancers are really poolside at the Siesta Cut-Rate Motel.

Permits

The First Amendment guarantees freedom of speech, and of the press, the free exercise of religion, the freedom for citizens to peaceably assemble and to petition the government for a redress of grievances. It does not, unfortunately, guarantee the right to show up wherever you want with a video crew and shoot a TV show without obtaining permission from the rightful owners. In the case of public spaces, like parks, streets, airports or the Department of Motor Vehicles, this means you have to get permission from the city, county, state or federal government agency in charge of that location.

Now I know some of you would like to make the case that you as a taxpayer are part-owner of all public things and, therefore, should be able to use your own property as a location for your project. But trust me — your friendly local police officer will not share your enlightened vision of communal resources. If he sees you and your actors and crew setting up in the middle of the street or outside the Amtrak station, he's going to ask to see your permit to film there. And if you don't have one to show him, he's going to ask you to leave. Immediately. Charm will do you no good. Neither will offering to bring him to the Oscars as your date when you are famous. Offers that involve greater personal sacrifice than that are strictly up to you, but they probably won't work, either.

If you want to film in a public space, especially if you have a crew beyond just yourself and more than one actor, you will need to get formal permission from the government entity that controls that space.

Developing A Shooting Schedule

If your series consists of a static webcam shot of you at your kitchen table riffing on which celebrity hottie you'd like to get busy with, then you don't really need a shooting schedule. Just sit down, hit RECORD and spew forth. If, however, you've written a script that calls for multiple scenes in various locations, then you need to figure out how long each of those segments will take to set up, light, rehearse and shoot. An hour? Five hours? Two days? And which hours or days? Are there only certain days or times when you have access to that location? Are certain times of day better or worse to shoot because of sunlight, traffic noise, or any of a dozen other factors? Do any of your actors have time restrictions — you know, like an actual paying job they might have to show up at? Each of these factors must be taken into consideration when determining your shooting schedule.

This may be ridiculously obvious to most of you in this media-savvy age, but it's worth pointing out that the scenes in movies and TV shows are rarely shot in the same order in which they appear in the script. The scenes are shuffled and regrouped so they can be photographed in the most efficient manner possible. If your script begins and ends in the desert, but has a scene by the ocean in between, it wouldn't make sense to drive out to the desert, shoot Scene 1, pack up the equipment and cast, drive to the ocean to shoot Scene 2, then drive back to the desert for Scene 3. You'd group the first and last scenes together and shoot them one right after the other, then pack up and head for the beach — or hit the beach the following day.

So how do you figure out the most efficient way to organize your shoot? The first step is to break your shoot down into its component parts, scene by scene. Though there are professional software programs that Hollywood production managers use to help with this task, it's probably overkill to invest the time and money in elaborate software when you can get the job done just fine with a pencil and some index cards.

At the top of each index card, write the name or "slugline" of each scene, like this:

INT. BEDROOM — NIGHT

Or this:

EXT. BEACH — DAY

Below the slugline, make two lists, side by side. List 1 — the cast members required for the scene. List 2 — any other crucial factors or components of the scene; e.g., "location available after 6 p.m. only" or "boa constrictor" or "Eddie in drag." At the bottom of the card, estimate how long you think it will take to shoot the scene. On the back of the card, write a one-sentence description to remind you of the essence of the scene, such as "The boa constrictor strangles Eddie at the beach."

Now spread the cards out in front of you and begin to organize them into sensible groups for shooting. What constitutes a "sensible grouping" is largely dictated by common sense. For instance, you might start by putting all the scenes that take place at the most frequently seen location in one column — say all the scenes that take place at your main character's home. Then look at the remaining scenes and see how they group. Just the café and the hardware store? Put them together and make a mental note that you'll need to find these two sites close to each other if possible.

Now look at each of your groups or columns and add up the total of estimated shoot time on each of the cards in that group. If it's your main character's house you might have:

```
INT. BEDROOM — DAY
(3 HOURS)

INT. BEDROOM — NIGHT
(2 HOURS)

EXT. BACKYARD — DAY
(4 HOURS)
```

That's a total of nine hours estimated. Let's say you're shooting in November in Los Angeles. You know you only have about nine hours of daylight so you probably wouldn't want to add any more scenes than this to be shot in one day. And you'd probably want to start first thing in the morning by shooting the exterior scene rather than shooting it last. Why? Because your time estimates for the interiors are just that — estimates. You need sunlight for that backyard scene and don't want to take a chance that the interiors will unexpectedly eat up so much time that you lose the light and end up having to come back to that location an additional day to complete the outside work. On the other hand, if the backyard takes a little longer than expected, no biggie. The last scene you're shooting that day is INT. BEDROOM — NIGHT. If it's dark outside, fine. If not, just tape black cloth over the windows outside. You're good to go either way.

Revising The Script To Fit The Logistics

Sometimes, when you put together your shooting schedule, some of the pieces just won't fit properly. You've only got half a day's work at the main house, and the scene that would be perfect to fill that other half day is the lunch scene at the café. Unfortunately, the café will only let you shoot on Mondays, when they are closed, and the house is only available on Tuesday, when your parents are out of town and you can film there despite the fact that they said you couldn't.

What's a producer to do?

A good producer runs through all the options, and then decides on the optimum choice. Among the options:

- Find a different house or café so they can be shot on the same day.
- Rewrite the café scene to a picnic lunch in the park, because there's a park right near the house that could be shot on Tuesday.
- Convince your parents that the sooner they let you shoot in the house on Monday the sooner you'll be able to make this pilot and use it to help you get a real paying job whereupon you can move out of the house, support yourself, and stop being a drain on their retirement savings.

In most cases, Hell will freeze over before Option #3 works. Option #1 is a possibility, but not always easy or available on demand at any given time. The most likely scenario is that at some point during preproduction you will need to make adjustments to the script to accommodate the logistical realities of time, budget and availability. Even the pros making a hundred-million-dollar action film must pay homage to the Gods of Reality and tweak the script a bit here and there to make it more efficient from a production standpoint. So don't let it throw you if your script doesn't instantly and conveniently break down into perfectly organized shooting components. Just get creative again. Ask yourself how the problems can be solved, answer the question in several ways, and then pick the best possible solution. You'll be surprised how many times necessity is the mother of invention and your new idea — new location or other new approach to the scene — turns out to be even better than what you had originally scripted.

Making A Shot List

We all know how it goes. A bunch of people are coming over to your place for dinner. You rush out to the grocery store without making a list. After all, it's just spaghetti and salad, so how hard can that be? You grab a cart, the salad fixings, stuff to make that killer sauce you saw Emeril whip up on Food Network the other night, and a primo bottle of wine because your friends are bringing over a dead ringer for Megan Fox who saw your picture on Facebook and said, "Hmmm, nice." You grab two more bottles of the wine, speed through the checkout stand with visions of Megan dancing in your head. (Even if you're female and straight, this vision should work for you. We're talking Megan Freaking Fox.)

You get home and begin madly chopping ingredients, only to discover that you forgot to actually buy the spaghetti... and condoms... which doesn't really matter because two seconds later *ding dong* Megan and friends show up and find out all you've got is salad (with no avocado... shit, forgot that too) and sauce so you order pizza and the delivery guy turns out to be some buff dude from the gym that Megan is always smiling at and they laugh and laugh and laugh about finally meeting this way and exchange phone numbers and she spends the rest of the night talking about how she can't wait to jump his bones and complaining about no avocado in the salad.

The moral of the story is simple: *Only a schmuck fails to make a list.*

The same goes for shooting your pilot. You must make a shot list ahead of time. Failure to do so is a guarantee that you will forget a bunch of really important shots you need and will end up with the video equivalent of an incomplete meal.

Okay, so now you know why you need a shot list — and why you will never hook up with someone who looks like Megan Fox. *Duh.* The next question is *how do you put a shot list together?*

Good news! Your subconscious has been working on this all along and you didn't even know it. While you were writing your scenes, you were visualizing them, too — on that virtual movie screen in your mind. That picnic lunch scene that your wrote? Look back at the script now and you'll be amazed at how you'll begin to see the shots you need:

```
EXT.  PARK — DAY

Justin  and  Ashley  share  a  picnic  lunch,  spread
out  on  a  blanket  on  a  grassy  knoll.  A  mother
plays  with  her  toddler  nearby.
```

See, right there, right now, you are visualizing a shot or two. Maybe it's a wide shot, establishing the location, then a two-shot of the couple digging into their sandwiches. Maybe the wide shot is taken from up high, on top of the slide, to add drama and interest to the setting. Whatever the case, hit pause on your mental projector and WRITE THIS STUFF DOWN. NOW. ON A PIECE OF PAPER. I'M SERIOUS. DO IT. TO BEGIN YOUR SHOT LIST WRITE:

• Establishing shot of park, high angle from atop slide.
• Two-shot, Justin and Ashley unpack sandwiches.

As you write that second one down, you realize that you'll also want to see that two-shot at various times during the rest of the scene, not just as they unpack their sandwiches. So you go back and amend that second shot to:

• Two-shot, Justin and Ashley (entire scene).

Now release the pause button and let the rest of the scene play out on your mental screen:

```
                    JUSTIN
        I  put  avocado  on  the  sandwiches.

Ashley  nods.

                    JUSTIN
        Want  some  wine?

Ashley  shakes  her  head.
```

```
              JUSTIN
     It's supposed to be really good. This
     guy on the Food Network gave it like 92
     points and said...

              ASHLEY
          (blurts it out)
     I'm pregnant.
```

Justin stops enjoying his lunch. The toddler
kicks his ball into Justin's lap, races over to
retrieve it. On Justin's awkward expression:

CUT TO:

It doesn't matter right now what we cut to — we're just working on the shot list for this one scene. And now you no doubt
have visualized more shots than just the establishing and two-
shot. I'd imagine you've seen close-ups of both Justin and Ashley
for their dialogue and reactions. Put them on the list, right below
the other two shots.

But don't stop with merely writing down what your subconscious tosses onto your mental movie screen. Your conscious
artistic mind must also be a part of this process. Your conscious
mind might tell you that you need to set up the toddler with the
ball earlier in the scene if you want that final moment of Justin,
imagining himself as the father of a young child, to pay off. So
you add to your list:

• Cutaway — mother and toddler play with ball.

But is it just a cutaway; an omniscient, detached shot for the
benefit of the audience? Or is it better to make it Ashley looking
at the child, smiling wistfully? Yes, that's better. So you cross out
the cutaway and replace it with:

• Angle on Ashley, watching mother and toddler.
• Ashley's POV: mother and toddler play with ball.

Good. Now run through the scene again on your imaginary
movie screen. See it shot by shot — the high-angle establishing

shot, two-shot of your couple, Ashley smiling at the mom and kid, shot of them with the ball, then back to the close-ups of your two principals and the dialogue. What about the end of the scene? Is the close-up of Justin sufficient to emphasize his reaction? Or do you need other sizes? A push-in to a tighter close-up? Or maybe a looser single to include the kid toddling over to retrieve his ball from a stunned Justin. Whatever it is, WRITE IT DOWN ON YOUR SHOT LIST.

Do this with each and every scene in your script. Then go back and look at the index card you wrote up to put together your shooting schedule. Maybe you wrote down:

```
EXT. PARK — DAY
(1 HOUR)
```

One hour seemed adequate in theory to shoot a simple four-line scene with two people in natural light. But now that you really think about it, you realize you need more time to get that establishing shot, and the cutaway, and the different sizes or angles on Justin and Ashley. So you adjust your shooting schedule accordingly.

```
EXT. PARK — DAY
(2 HOURS)
```

Now look at the other work you have scheduled for the day you shoot that picnic scene. Does adding an extra hour to that day still work? If not, ask yourself how you can best solve the scheduling problem. Adjust the script? Simplify your shooting plan for one or more scenes? Add an extra day to your shooting schedule?

Your script, shot list and shooting schedule are all interrelated and preproduction is where you will constantly revise and adapt each of them to balance the competing demands of creativity versus physical and financial limitations.

Props And Wardrobe

Props and wardrobe are more than just the items the actors happen to wear or carry. They are windows into each of your characters, externalizations of their internal world, if you will. The way your characters appear on the outside tells us a great deal about who they are on the inside. In the movie *Big*, even though twelve-year-old Josh Baskin has been transformed into the adult body of Tom Hanks, he still chooses to furnish his "adult" apartment in Manhattan like the boy he is inside, with a bunk bed, trampoline, and a slew of pre-adolescent toys. In *Little Miss Sunshine*, the dysfunctional family travels to California in a barely functioning VW van which they can only start if they all push it together to get it rolling.

This isn't rocket science; it's just common sense in most cases. But props and wardrobe are all too often overlooked by newer filmmakers who squander this rich opportunity to add visual and character value to each scene. So take the time to ask yourself about the visual details for each of your characters. What would they wear? What kind of car would they drive? Or would they take the bus or a funky old bike? In most cases, the elements you need can be obtained for free, from your own closet, or the actor's, or at worst for a few dollars at a thrift shop.

Situations That Require Special Preproduction

It would be impossible to detail each and every situation that may demand preparation for your pilot. Stories and scenes come in all shapes, sizes and varieties, and therefore can have an infinite spectrum of preproduction needs. Nonetheless, these needs must be met and prepared for. So as you go through each scene preparing your shot list, also ask yourself if there are special elements that demand special preparation.

- Are there any scenes where one or more characters sing or sing to music? If so, you may want to prerecord these to get them just right, then have your characters lip-sync to a play-back track when you shoot the scene.

- Dance numbers also require significant preparation and rehearsal. If one or more of your characters dance, you will want to rehearse this segment ahead of time.
- Is there any special training called for? Martial arts moves? A fight scene? These types of scenes are choreographed ahead of time, with lots of rehearsal, just like a dance number.

As I said, the variations are endless, but as Sun Tzu said, all battles are won before they are fought. So think ahead and prepare.

● FOR TEACHERS...

Preproduction class sessions work best as Socratic workshops. Conduct an interrogative with the students. Ask how many days they plan to shoot (unless you are defining or limiting this your-self). Ask if they plan any rehearsal with the actors ahead of time. Most of all, ask them to put their plans down on paper, to prepare a shot list for each scene, then to take this shot list and make a "Time Management Budget" for each day — a docu-ment that takes the shot list and specifies how much time they are budgeting for each scene, for lunch, for company moves, etc.

This Time Management Budget is a most useful tool for dis-cussing whether the students have planned enough time for what they hope to accomplish. Instead of having an abstract discus-sion about whether they "feel" they can get everything done in the time allotted, the Time Management Budget breaks the ques-tion down into smaller, easier chunks to analyze. And because it contains not just the scenes they plan to shoot but their shot list for each of those scenes, it tends to bring the discussion into sharper focus. Instead of asking if they really feel they can shoot Scene 3 in an hour and a half, the question now becomes *Really? You think you can shoot Scene 3 — all 15 shots — in 90 min-utes? That's 6 minutes to set up, light, rehearse and shoot each shot on average. Do you really think you can accomplish that and give the actors and their performances the time and attention they deserve?* Confronted with this sort of evidence in black and white, most students are able to see when they have not planned properly and can make adjustments; e.g., schedule more time, condense the shot list, or some combination of the two. Putting the Time Management Budget down on paper helps train the students to previsualize their shooting days and to spot problems more effectively ahead of time.

Another helpful preproduction class exercise is guiding the students through one or more production meetings. Teach them how to talk through the production elements of the script, going through it scene by scene, page by page, with the student director leading the discussion and defining her needs along the way (props, extras, special lighting elements, etc.) and urging the other students to chime in and ask questions along the way regarding their particular area of responsibility; e.g., *How do you see her dressed for this date?* or *Are you going to cast the barista who keeps smiling at her or should I just find a good-looking extra for that?*

The goal, as always, is to get the students to simulate the process that professionals would go through. Even if the script is only two pages long, practicing professional process trains the students to think and behave like professionals.

CHAPTER TEN
THE PILOT – PRODUCTION

It's finally here! The day you've been waiting for since that first flash of inspiration for your series popped into your head — the day you arrive on location with the actors and begin shooting your pilot. And because you've put so much time and effort into preparing for this day — writing and rewriting the script until it's exactly what you want, finding the perfect cast, visualizing each scene and building your shot list and Time Management Budget, going over each and every detail ahead of time — now it practically shoots itself, proceeding exactly as planned without a hiccup, right?

Well... no.

Despite the sage advice of Coach Wooden and Sun Tzu about the importance of preparation, there is another bit of timeless wisdom that inevitably comes into play when the planning stops and actual production begins. There is dispute about who first codified the wisdom, but no argument about its fundamental truth. Written in the original Old English, the advice goes like this:

𝔖𝔥𝔦𝔱 𝔥𝔞𝔭𝔭𝔢𝔫𝔰.

Dealing With The Unexpected

No matter how thoroughly you prepare, you must also be ready to deal with the unexpected. Curveballs that may be thrown your way can include:

- Equipment failure.
- An actor gets a new idea for the scene.
- You get a new idea for the scene.
- When you rehearse the scene you realize your shot list is flawed and needs to be amended.
- You didn't realize this was the day the city would begin demolition on the street outside your location.
- An intergalactic war breaks out and the Remulons have landed their battle cruisers right in the middle of your quiet picnic scene in the park.

With the possible exception of that last one, somehow the shoot must go on. No matter what kind of lemons the Video Gods chuck at you, you'll need to stay calm, think clearly, dismiss the urge to curl up in a ball and weep, consider your options, and figure out your best course of action given whatever new circumstances you've been presented with. The good news is that making movies is alchemy, so the curveball you're thrown might actually lead not to disaster but to creative inspiration. As often as not, Plan B turns out to be far superior to Plan A. Best of all, no one watching the final product will ever know that Plan B was pulled out of your ass at the last minute; they'll think you had it figured that way all along.

A prime example of Plan B superiority is the movie *Jaws*, about a super-sized shark that terrorizes a beach town. Since sharks are notoriously bad at performing on cue, the film required the use of a mechanical shark. A bunch of Hollywood special effects wizards built one and nicknamed it Bruce. Alas, Bruce was not a show-biz natural and did not perform exactly as planned. The first time they lowered him into the water on location, he promptly sank to the ocean floor. A team of divers retrieved Bruce and made him seaworthy, but the darn thing just never quite worked right. Even worse, when it appeared on camera for more than a brief glimpse it looked kind of cheesy. So director Steven Spielberg considered his options and made lemonade out of the lemons he'd been handed. Instead of featuring Bruce prominently on camera, as originally planned, he used subjective camera and put us, the audience, into the shark's point of view, stalking victims from under the water, laying in wait, poised to attack.

It was a brilliant solution. Though at the time this may have seemed like a compromise, it turned out to be by far the stronger creative choice. The scariest moments in this thriller are when we *don't* see the shark. The less we see it, the more frightening the monster is in our minds. We'll never know for sure, but my suspicion is that if Bruce had worked exactly as planned, and Spielberg showed him to us over and over and over again, the film might have turned out to be a laughable B-movie instead of the classic that it is.

Coping with the unpredictable is an entirely predictable part of the job of making a video. So when the lemon yogurt hits the fan, don't panic. Just smile and deal with it. If you want certainty and guarantees, there's a cubicle right next to Dilbert waiting for you. If you want to make TV shows, get used to the fact that life is what happens while you're making other plans.

Be Quick, But Don't Hurry

This ironic instruction is yet another of Coach Wooden's famous pearls of wisdom. As with many of Wooden's sayings, it applies to far more than just basketball. For instance, it's great advice for anyone shooting an Internet TV pilot on a tight schedule. Production is, in a sense, game day for filmmakers. The quiet contemplation of preproduction is replaced by the frenzied pressure cooker of actually committing your plans to video while the clock is ticking and sunlight is fading. Maybe you only have permission to be at the location for two hours. Or perhaps the actor you cast has to leave for his paying job by 2 p.m. Or you've got to finish this scene in the next thirty minutes because that's when the bulldozers start up again in the empty lot next door. Pressure, pressure, pressure.

The only way you'll get the day's work done is by being quick. But the last thing you want to do is hurry. Being quick means being thoughtful but decisive. Hurrying is when you just blurt out any old answer to make the question go away. Being quick means being efficient, and staying focused on the task at hand without getting bogged down hemming and hawing about insignificant or extraneous things. Hurrying is careless, unfocused, frenetic activity which inevitably leads to inefficiency.

A corollary to "Be Quick, But Don't Hurry" is "Have Fun, But Stay Businesslike." Shooting a pilot is tons of fun. You're seeing something you dreamed up become a reality. You're more than likely working with some of your best friends. If you're shooting a comedy — well, what's not fun about laughing all day long at work? But that last word is key — you're at work. So laugh, joke, have fun — but remember that there's a job to be done. There's a fine line between keeping things loose on the set and letting things fall apart. It's important to have a sense of always staying on the happy but focused and productive side of that line.

Getting Enough Takes And Coverage

There are some situations where not only shouldn't you hurry, but you shouldn't worry about being all that quick either. When it comes to making sure you've got all the footage you need before you move on from one shot or one scene to the next, taking a few moments to ask *Do I really have everything I'll need?* is much more important than rushing forward at warp speed. There's nothing worse than getting in the editing room and discovering that you really don't have all the pieces you need to cut that scene together the way you imagined. Well, okay, being eaten alive by a pack of wild hyenas is probably worse. So is an anesthetic-free colonoscopy. But realizing that you forgot to get all the shots you need, then being forced to put the scene together in editing without a key ingredient is its own form of agony.

Even if you've followed your shot list religiously, you must still run the scene on that imaginary flatscreen in your mind and make sure you have everything you need in the can. Funny things happen to the movie in your mind when you shift from the speculative phase of preproduction and shoot the scene with real actors on a real location. The movie can change. Maybe you saw it all in a two-shot in your mind when you drew up your shot list, but now you're seeing close-ups as well. Your shot list didn't call for close-ups to be shot. But now your gut is telling you that you might want them. LISTEN TO YOUR GUT. It's not that you necessarily made a mistake when putting together the shot list. It's just that now you have more information to work with and this new info is telling you to get more coverage.

You may also find that the movie in your mind "flickers" or is blurry on certain issues. Sometimes you see a certain moment in a two-shot, sometimes in close-up. So you find yourself uncertain as to whether you really need that close-up or not. My advice is simple: *When in doubt, shoot it*. You're there at the location, you've got the equipment and the actors, and it'll only take a few more minutes. Maybe you won't use it in the end. But having an extra shot or two is a whole lot better than trying to put the jigsaw puzzle together during editing only to discover that you forgot to collect some crucial pieces.

The same principle applies to evaluating whether you've got enough takes of a given shot. Have you really gotten the performance you wanted? All the way through the scene? Or is there a line the actor always flubbed? Again, better to take a few extra minutes and shoot it again, even if you end up using take one in the final edit, than to get into the editing room and kick yourself for never shooting take two.

One final note on this: it's video, so do yourself a favor and play it back and watch it if you're unsure whether you have everything you need. Sometimes what you thought happened on camera isn't what actually happened. This is because our mind tends to only see what it expects to see. For instance, Harvard psychology professor Daniel Simons conducted an experiment where people were asked to watch a video of two teams of basketball players passing a basketball back and forth. One team wore white shirts, the other team wore black shirts. Viewers were asked to count how many times players on one team passed the ball, but to ignore the other team. After the viewers finished watching the tape, they were asked questions about how many passes their assigned team had made, plus one other simple question: *When did the gorilla come on screen?* About half the viewers never saw any gorilla — and were stunned when the tape was played back and they could plainly see that about halfway through, a person in a gorilla suit walked in front of the camera, beat his chest, then walked off. They never saw the gorilla because they weren't looking for a gorilla. Scientists call this "inattentional blindness." Similarly, when you're shooting, you're watching the actors, evaluating their performance. You may not see all kinds of things that have unexpectedly crept into your shot — lights, microphones, passersby staring into the camera, and so on.

So you can't always rely on your "in the moment" vision to perceive what shouldn't be in your shot. But the tape doesn't lie. It captures exactly what happened in that moment, even if you missed the gorilla.

By the way, for those of you who might be thinking *How the hell can you not see a freaking gorilla?*, just type "Gorillas in our Midst Daniel Simons" into a search engine and you can read the study yourself.

Finally, the fact that Professor Simons' study was called "Gorillas in our Midst" proves that even ivory tower academics know the value of a catchy title.

You Aren't the Only Genius On The Set

Milton Berle, dubbed Mr. Television in the late 1940s because of the phenomenal success of his variety show, once said, "I know a good joke when I steal one." Amen to that. Yes, this little pilot you're making is "your baby." But everybody else involved can love your baby, too. They are its aunts and uncles and want nothing more than to help your baby be all he can be. So if anyone, from the star right on down to the guy at the donut shop, has a good idea for something that will add to your project, for God's sake do what any self-respecting artist would do and use that idea.

Among other things, this means you must *listen* to the people around you. It also means you have to create an atmosphere where the cast and crew feel welcome to contribute creatively. If suggestions by the crew are constantly met with an exasperated sigh or steely glare, that tends to be the end of those suggestions even being floated. And that, my friend, is your loss.

This doesn't mean you have to accept or include every notion thrown your way. But it does mean that the spirit and general attitude on your set should be "Ideas Welcome." When the mechanical shark failed, coping with the situation by replacing shots of the shark with shots from the shark's POV was an ingenious solution. Does it really matter whether this idea came from Spielberg or from the cinematographer or whomever? The bottom line is Spielberg had the good sense to recognize this as a great idea and to use it in his film.

Actors Aren't Puppets

One of the biggest challenges for novice directors, especially those who also wrote the script, is learning how to collaborate effectively with actors. Working with actors is a subject worthy of entire books. In fact, here are two you might want to read in preparation for your shoot: *Directing Actors* by Judith Weston, and *Respect For Acting* by Uta Hagen with Haskel Frankel.

In the meantime, suffice it to say that actors aren't puppets and you won't get good performances from them if you treat them as such. You can't manipulate their every vocal inflection or facial tic. As much as you may feel this is your baby and you've seen each character's performance on that movie screen in your mind and that's the way it must be, you have to let the actors do their work. This doesn't mean that you just sit back and let them veer off in whatever improvised direction they feel like. But it does mean that you can't micromanage their performance.

A good rule of thumb is this: talk with the actors about their goals and motivations in the scene (as in "you're flirting, you want him to like you"), but don't try to tell the actors what specific techniques they should use to achieve that goal (as in "bat your eyelashes when you say that, then giggle"). You wouldn't (and shouldn't) try to tell a cinematographer what kind of lights to use or where to put them. Those are his professional choices, based on his expertise. You'd simply say, "I'd like it to be dark and mysterious looking in this scene." Give the actors the same courtesy and professional acknowledgement. Let them do what they are trained to do.

If there are occasions where you feel the need to direct physicality, float the suggestion as an idea, not a directive. For example, you might say, "It feels like you might want to lean closer to him starting in this part of the scene." This gives the actor the freedom to hear what you want but find a way to accomplish that end result in his own way, by either internalizing that suggestion and making it his own or by finding another route to the same destination.

Crewmembers Aren't Slaves

Human beings have an amazing capacity to connect and identify personally with the work they do. When the Lakers win the NBA championship, the guy who sells peanuts in the nosebleed section still thinks to himself *Yeah, baby, we did it, we're number 1!* The part-time barista at Starbucks #5782 thinks of it as *our* coffee not *their* coffee.

When it comes to the crew of a movie or TV show, you can take that emotional identification and multiply it by ten. Every single person who works on your project will think of it as *our* pilot.

This is a gift from the gods. It means the crew working with you will bust their collective booties to make sure that it's the best pilot it can be. So the very least you can do, whether you are paying your crew or not, is to treat them with the utmost courtesy, respect, consideration and admiration. Notice what they are doing and say something about it. If somebody contributes a small detail — a lighting effect, or a piece of wardrobe or a prop — that adds texture or value to your pilot, then take the five seconds to say, "I love that sweater you picked for her. It's *so* perfect for the character."

It's also important to remember that if something is taking longer than you want it to, or if a crewmember is struggling with a faulty piece of equipment, they are just as frustrated as you are. Sniping and huffing at the sound mixer as if he caused the mixing deck to go south on purpose is not only a crappy way to act, it's actually counterproductive. Let the guy do his work and fix the problem. The more understanding you are during moments of adversity, the harder the crew will work for you when the problem does get fixed and you're pressed for time because of the delay.

It's a Golden Rule thing: *Do unto others as you would want them to do unto you.* Speaking for myself, I work much harder for people who tell me I'm great than for people who are always critical or indifferent.

Another Golden Rule for treating your cast and crew properly is *always feed them well.* No matter how small your budget is or how pressed for funds you are, you've got to make sure that you've got donuts and bagels in the morning, water and soda at all times, and provide decent meals at the meal break times. If you've got vegetarians, make sure they've got what they need, too. A well-fed crew is a happy crew, and a happy crew is a productive crew.

To paraphrase a well-known ad:
Bagels and cream cheese: ten dollars.
Pizza for eight: twenty-two fifty.
A loyal crew: priceless.

The World Is Not A Set

Movies and TV have an amazing capacity to make the nonexistent seem real. Watch *Men In Black* and you happily give yourself over to the notion that aliens live among us and the only reason we're in the dark about it is because of a secret government agency that owns a flashy-thingy device that zaps the memories right out of your brain. Watch 24 and you eagerly buy into the notion that Jack Bauer can single-handedly defeat terrorism while never encountering traffic of any kind in Los Angeles. That's the power of the moving image: even the wildly improbable seems real.

Ironically, when you're involved in the making of the moving image, you're so immersed in the process of turning fantasy into reality that you tend to forget about actual reality. You start believing that all the world's a set, and all its people merely extras waiting for you to point them in the right direction.

Alas, such is not life. Locations are not just settings to serve your dramatic needs — they are real places where real people will live and work long after you've wrapped. Miraculously, ordinary folks have generously allowed you to disrupt their home or business so you can shoot your scene. Often they have done this for free, out of the goodness of their hearts. The very least you can do is to treat their place with courtesy and respect. This means you take care not to damage anything, clean up your trash at the end of the day, and make sure to restore the property to the way it was before you and your crew descended upon it like locusts. This is not only common decency — it's smart business. You may want to come back someday and film this location again. The people who own the location tend to be more open to this request when you haven't burned a hole in their rug.

If you're shooting in a public setting, you will inevitably need to deal with that public. This can be inconvenient; people may stand or wander where you don't want them to, and you'll need to ask them to move. But there's a right way and a wrong way to do this. The right way would be something like *I'm sorry folks but we need to ask you to move over there. Thanks for helping us, we really appreciate it.* The wrong way would be *Okay you idiots are in my shot and need to move NOW! That means you, fatass!* As a general rule of thumb, you want to sound like Mary Poppins, not Dick Cheney.

Another thing to remember when you're immersed in the make believe of making movies is that the real world still has real physical consequences. Fire is hot. Knives are sharp. Those cars and busses in the street are not pretend props from a *Looney Tunes* cartoon. If you step in front of them, you will not be humorously flattened into a funny pancake version of yourself. You will be maimed or killed.

Always remember that the laws of nature take precedence over the magic of movies. Keep yourself, your cast and crew safe at all times. If I sound like your mother here... then you probably had a good mother. Call her once in a while and send her something nice for Mother's Day this year, not that lame e-card at the last minute.

● FOR TEACHERS...

To be or not to be on the set, that is the central question for teachers during the production phase. Whether 'tis nobler to let them sink or swim entirely on their own, and learn from their mistakes, or to provide guidance in the moment as they work through their production day. The choice is ultimately yours, and there really isn't, IMHO, a right or wrong answer to the question.

The "hands off" advocates make a strong case for allowing the students to make their film, not the teacher's version of the student's film. They also make a valid point that having the teacher present inevitably changes the power dynamic on the set. Instead of the student director or creator being the creative center of gravity, the teacher can't help but draw focus to himself, undercutting the director or creator's obligation and responsibility to be the final word on things, thereby diluting the experience.

On the other hand, my colleague James Gardner is a strong believer that the teacher's presence adds greatly to the learning experience provided that presence is a Socratic one — one that poses questions that might not have occurred to the students for them to think through and answer. *Why do you feel you need this shot? Are you sure you have enough coverage? We only have time to shoot three of the four remaining shots on your list — which shots are the most important to you?*

As I said, both approaches have value and pedagogical substance. And you needn't pick one method and stick with it for life. Experiment with both, and use whichever suits you and your particular student population best.

CHAPTER ELEVEN
THE PILOT – POSTRODUCTION

Editing has often been called the final rewrite. It's where you find out whether the movie you imagined in your head is the one you shot, and if it works on a real screen as well as it did on the virtual one in your mind. When it does, it can be thrilling, like pulling off a magic trick. When it doesn't... well, just like in production, necessity is often the mother of invention. You may not be able to assemble the pieces quite the way you imagined, but sometimes that's a good thing. Sometimes you suddenly see a moment or a scene or even the whole story in a new, inspired way and create something different than what you had in mind originally, something even more exciting. Just as with Transformers (the toys, not the movie), the pieces that made a fire truck, when reshuffled, can also form a really cool dragon.

None of this is meant to imply that you should automatically abandon your script and just start improvising during the editing phase. Or that you can now take what you've shot and make whatever movie strikes your fancy, suddenly taking what was meant to be a romantic comedy about a couple in their twenties and somehow twisting that into a sci-fi horror flick about a planet where everyone has three heads — their own, Rush Limbaugh's and Michael Moore's (how scary is that?). It does, however, mean that editing is not a paint-by-numbers process where you mindlessly assemble your footage exactly as your shot list and script called for. You must take a fresh look at everything and ask yourself if there might be a better way to organize or present things.

As with cinematography, sound, directing and other areas we've covered, the art and craft of editing are subjects we can't possibly explore thoroughly in one short chapter. The principles, techniques and philosophy of editing are subjects worthy of entire books. Fortunately, a bunch have been written. I encourage you to read the ones listed in Appendix 2 if you are new to editing and want a more thorough education on the subject. In fact, even if you aren't new to editing, check them out. They will inspire you and expand your skills and talents as an editor and filmmaker.

The Rough Cut — Putting It Together

Before you even begin to edit, you must watch all the footage you shot to arm yourself with a basic familiarity with what you've got. Yes, I know, you were there when you shot it. But watch everything again, every single shot, every single take, to refresh your memory. Sometimes memory plays funny tricks and we forget that take where the actor did something really wonderful with that one line, or forget that other angle we shot. The human mind retains only a tiny fraction of what it is exposed to — and that fraction is even smaller if you drank too much at the wrap party. So be disciplined and watch every frame you shot before making any decisions about how to put it together.

Furthermore, as you watch the raw footage you shot (known as "dailies"), you should make notes. Every pilot is different, but a typical three- to five-minute webisode could easily have fifty or sixty different angles, with multiple takes on each setup. Even the Amazing Kreskin couldn't possibly remember every frame of that. You can save yourself a lot of editing time by jotting down a few reminders for each take. Let's say you shot four takes of the master shot for Scene 1. Using the shorthand "1,1" for Scene 1, Take 1, your notes might look like this:

1,1 — good performances, mike dips in and out
1,2 — John good, Mary so-so in second half
1,3 — John bobbles "cheesecake" line
1,4 — Mary bobbles last line

Now, when you go to edit Scene 1, and you want to use the master angle for a section for the scene, you have some clues about where to look and where not to look.

• • •

After you have watched all the dailies and written notes for yourself, you will begin the process of assembling a rough cut. As the word "rough" indicates, this is not intended to be anything close to a polished, perfected, ready-for-broadcast version of your pilot. It is, like the first draft of your script, a way to put it all together in concrete form so you can evaluate what you have, see what works, and see what needs to be improved or fixed. The rough cut is not the time to finesse or obsess over fine points. That comes later. For now, just cut the scenes together in a way that makes basic sense to you — probably fairly close to the way you imagined it when you put your shot list together. The reason you don't want to spend a lot of time on polishing at this point is that you need to view the rough cut first and get a sense of "the big picture." Does the story work? Are the characters clear? Are there places that seem redundant or that feel slow? Maybe there are things that need to be edited out — perhaps even entire scenes — which is why you shouldn't polish the editing to a fare-thee-well during the rough cut phase. If you spend hours and hours getting Scene 1 exactly right, frame by frame, then watch your cut and discover that Scene 1 is superfluous and you can really get the whole story moving a lot faster by dropping Scene 1 and beginning with Scene 2... well, you wasted an awful lot of time perfecting something that will never see the light of day with an audience.

In general, you will want to keep the amount of postproduction sound work you do to a minimum until you have "locked picture" — made the final decisions and edits on the video content. The reason for this is the same as above — why spend time fixing the sound on a line of dialogue that may never end up in the final version?

The Rough Cut — Assessing What You Have

Okay, you've watched all the dailies, made your notes, and put together your rough cut. Put it away for at least twenty four hours (to gain some distance and perspective), then sit down and watch it all the way through. In my experience, most people, if they are honest with themselves, will have some version of the following reaction to watching their rough cut: *This is a complete freaking mess, utterly beyond repair. I'd like to throw up on my shoes, then burn all this footage so no one will ever see what a no-talent hack I am.*

This is a completely normal reaction. Not fun, but normal. Take a deep breath or two and repeat after me: *This is a **rough cut**. Everybody's rough cut sucks. It's just part of the process.*

When you've stopped dry heaving, do the unthinkable and watch your rough cut all the way through once again. When you've done that, get out your pad of paper and write some "big picture" notes. Maybe you want to drop a scene, or parts of some scenes. Or maybe the story sags in the middle, but in watching the film twice now, it has suddenly occurred to you that those two minutes will work much better as a 30-second montage with music pushing it along than as three flat-footed, bloated dialogue scenes. Again, every project will be different, but for now, write down whatever seems wrong to you and any ideas you have for fixing what seems wrong.

Now watch your rough cut one more time, but this time break it down into smaller pieces; start and stop it wherever something seems off. Ask yourself what seems wrong and what sort of editing approach might help. Jot this down, then hit PLAY and keep watching until the next bump in the road.

When you finish this process, even if you haven't figured out quite how to solve all the problems, it's time to leave the rough cut and move on to Cut #2.

One final rough cut note: you may be tempted at this point in time to screen what you've got for someone, frequently your significant other. DON'T DO IT. They won't like it, because it's a rough cut and nobody likes rough cuts. I know, I know — your S.O. is dying to see it. And you've been living with it alone for a long time and are dying for someone to see what you've invested all this time and energy on and say *Wow, that's really great!* DO NOT GIVE IN TO THIS URGE AND SCREEN THE ROUGH CUT FOR AN OUTSIDER. It can only bring you pain and self-doubt. Why? Because no matter how loudly and often you say "This is just a rough cut," when a person watches something, he can't help but evaluate it as if it's a finished product, like every other video product he's seen at the movies, on TV and on the Internet. He will react as if you put flour, eggs, tomato sauce, mozzarella and ricotta cheese, ground beef and spices in front of him and said, "How do you like my lasagna?" He'll look at you in great pain, wanting to be nice, but will only be able to say, "Well... I don't know... I guess it just doesn't look like lasagna to me." Where you see potential, he will only see unassembled, unfinished raw ingredients. And worst of all, his doubt and concern will leap through the air, reach into your chest, and suck the heart right out of you. Lack of enthusiasm is incredibly contagious, and it's the last thing you need right now. What you need is to somehow set aside your burning desire for praise, do your editing work, and wait until you've got a finished product before showing it to anyone.

Refining The Cut

Okay, you've watched your rough cut, made your notes, and had sex with your S.O. because you wisely refrained from screening the rough cut for her and avoided a big fight about her lack of enthusiasm. You're welcome. Now your job is to take the rough cut and start improving it, moving it closer to being a final product.

Notice I said closer to being a final product, not all the way there. As with your script, editing demands the patience to go through multiple versions — a second, third, fourth and fifth cut. It is a painstaking process that requires sustained focus on each and every detail. The good news is that your spirits will rise with each successive cut. As predictable as it is that you will want to vomit after watching your rough cut, it's also a solid bet that upon screening your second cut you'll quietly say to yourself *Hey, this isn't half bad. In fact, it's kind of good.*

My students go through this emotional roller coaster time and again. I ask them how their shoot went and they're giddy with excitement — can't wait to see it all cut together. Then we dim the lights and screen the editor's rough cut. When the lights go up, the room is filled with... uncomfortable silence. Maybe even shame and humiliation. Their faces say *I thought it was good, but maybe I just don't have what it takes.* I help them through the moment and remind them it's just a rough cut. We screen it again, scene by scene, starting and stopping to discuss how and where improvements are needed. But the nauseous discomfort of the rough cut screening stays with them... until our next class session when the editor screens a revised cut and *Hallelujah! It is healed!* Still not perfect, but a gazillion times better than the rough cut. It's actually starting to look like lasagna!

You may be tempted to call it done at this point, eager to slap in a little music and some quick titles and post it on YouTube. After all, you've worked really hard on this pilot, think it's pretty darn good, and want to share it with the world. Don't do it. Not yet. You're not quite done. This is a good time to go back through the books you've read for guidance on editing. Maybe you'll want to review the chapters on editing dialogue, or on pace, or whatever other areas may apply to your pilot. While the books obviously won't comment on your particular project, they will very likely stimulate your thinking about it. They can inspire you to take another look at each scene with a fresh eye, and can help you bring the quality of the edit — and, therefore, the quality of the finished product — up another notch or two.

Postproduction Sound

In life, there are certain tasks which always seem to drift to the bottom of the "To Do" list. Cleaning the bathroom. Going to the dentist. Doing your taxes. For those over fifty, getting a colonoscopy. None of these activities are much fun, but all are necessary. Pretending otherwise is simply a recipe for your daily life taking a turn for the worse.

So, too, with postproduction sound. It is among the most thankless, tedious, time-consuming parts of making a film. It is also among the elements that instantly separate a sloppy, amateurish pilot from a polished, professional effort. Nothing takes an audience out of a story faster than half-assed sound work. All of your hard work creating the premise and characters, writing a witty, well-constructed script, and shooting great performances with brilliant camera angles will be totally lost on the audience if their main reaction to the piece is *What's wrong with the sound?*

So once you've gone through the process of refining the edit several times, and have "locked picture" — meaning you are totally satisfied with each and every visual moment of your pilot — it's time to go to work on the audio. Here are some of the main tasks you must tackle:

- **Clarity**. Is each and every line of dialogue clear and understandable to the audience? Remember: they haven't read the script, so the only way they can understand what is being said is if they can hear it clearly. Sometimes the actor's best overall performance during a given moment includes a garbled line. You can still use the video performance you want *if* you do one of two things to fix the sound: a) steal the audio from a different take or even a different shot of the same moment and "stick it in the actor's mouth" — or b) bring the actor in and have a dialogue replacement or "looping" session.

- **Balance**. You shot a dinner scene between two people. But the sound levels on the two close-ups don't match. One is much louder than the other, even though in the scene they are speaking at approximately the same level. You need to adjust one or both levels to get them to match.
- **Ambience**. Ambient sound is a key element in establishing and reinforcing a sense of place and time. If your scene is set at a sleazy motel in a bad part of town, you can emphasize this by adding sirens, gunshots, barking dogs, sounds of a couple arguing next door, etc. All of these can add texture to your scene, though they must also have proper:
- **Perspective**. If the couple next door is arguing, they need to sound muffled, as if there is a wall and distance between them and the camera; they shouldn't sound like they are right there in the room with your actors. Similarly, if you've filmed a scene at a romantic café overlooking the ocean, you might want to add the muted sound of waves breaking on the beach. But this must be done with perspective, unless you want the audience to think your love-struck couple is in the middle of *The Perfect Storm*.

For specific instruction on techniques for accomplishing any of the tasks above, consult one of the sound books in Appendix 2.

Adding Music

This is the one part of postproduction sound that's actually a ton of fun. Nothing brings a film alive faster than a great soundtrack. That montage of your couple falling in love — the one you were starting to have second thoughts about — suddenly soars with romance when a great song is playing behind it. And that action sequence you shot, the one that never quite seemed to work as well as you imagined, suddenly crackles with heart-pounding excitement when a throbbing music track pulses throughout. We are, I believe, so conditioned from years of watching movies and TV with great soundtracks that films without any music seem oddly incomplete.

Try to imagine this: the shark attack scenes in *Jaws* without that haunting, make the hair on the back of your neck stand up *dum-dum dum-dum dum-dum* music underneath. They just wouldn't be as scary. Or imagine a great romantic comedy, building to the climactic moment when our couple finally gets together and kisses... but with no music. They kiss, credits against black, all in silence. I'd venture to say that no music = no emotional payoff = unsatisfied audience.

But where do you get the music from? You probably don't have the budget or contacts to allow you to fire off a quick text message asking Beyoncé if she'd be willing to write and record something for you. And if you're thinking you can just pull a song off her latest CD and drop it into your soundtrack... well, there's this pesky thing called copyright law that may get in your way. Yes, I know, many people make use of copyrighted music without permission for their videos on YouTube. But this isn't strictly legal, merely overlooked in most cases due to the sheer volume of material and the fact that most of it isn't posted for commercial purposes. If you want to post on sites beyond YouTube, or create your own site, and have any intention of selling your series to someone, or sharing in online ad revenue, then you cannot use copyrighted music without obtaining the rights to do so — and those rights are typically many thousands of dollars.

So where can you obtain affordable music to use for wider, commercial purposes? Several places. First, just as you are an aspiring videomaker, hoping to be discovered on the Internet, the Web is filled with aspiring musicians. Surf the Net, find an "up and comer" with a song you'd like to use, and contact that person. Explain what you want, offer a prominent screen credit in exchange for use of the music, and — without overselling — suggest that perhaps the exposure your pilot and series will garner may also attract new fans and paying customers for the musician's CDs. You may even try offering a nominal fee — say fifty dollars — or offer to buy some of the artist's CDs. If the musician says no, so be it. But one of the unwritten rules of producing low-budget, creative work is that if you ask nicely, they might say yes. But if you don't ask, the answer is always no.

A second avenue to obtain quality music might be to approach a local musician, someone playing in a coffee house or book store, whose musical style fits the needs of your pilot. Again, try to present this as an opportunity for the musician to trade his services and talents for exposure to a wider audience. He's already playing for little or no money hoping the fifty folks in the coffee house might buy some CDs. Even if your pilot only gets five thousand hits, incredibly modest for YouTube or other major sites, this would be equivalent exposure to one hundred nights of playing live to fifty people.

Finally, let's not ignore the direct route. Perhaps you actually play a musical instrument yourself. You don't have to be Eric Clapton, but if you play well enough and can write a bit of appropriate music you might be able to fill in the transitions and other short musical needs. One word of caution: just because you're playing the music (or singing) yourself DOES NOT give you the right to cover your favorite hit song and use it for commercial purposes in your pilot. Both the original performance AND the writing of the song are covered by copyright law.

Creating A Main Title

I used to work for Tom Miller, one of the most successful producers in the history of television. Tom's shows include *Happy Days, Laverne & Shirley, Bosom Buddies, Mork & Mindy, Perfect Strangers, Full House, Family Matters*, and the show I helped write and produce, *Step By Step*. Among other gifts, Tom had a fierce passion for main titles. And I bet that if you've seen any of the shows listed above even a few times, you can instantly recall the main title — the smiling cast framed by a spinning 1950s record in *Happy Days*, or Laverne and Shirley hop-skipping to "schlemiel, schlimazel, hasenpfeffer incorporated," etc. On *Step By Step*, it was the family going on the rollercoaster ride, at an amusement park right on the shore of Lake Michigan (this amusement park doesn't exist and was created by photographing an inland park and adding the water through visual effects in postproduction.) The show ran for seven years, during which time the number one question I was asked by fans was "Is there really an amusement park right by the water? I want to go there."

Some people felt that Tom's passion for main titles ran to obsession, that it was a waste of time and money out of step with the changing face of television, where main titles were getting shorter and less elaborate. Even Tom eventually agreed that the longest of the main titles (the original version of the *Step By Step* main title ran well over a minute and a half) could use some tightening. But he refused to do what many shows were beginning to do — reduce the main title to a simple title card, then run the credits for the series stars over the action and dialogue of the beginning of the episode. Why did Tom Miller resist this growing trend? Because he knew that no matter how much TV changed, you only get one chance to make a first impression, and that first impressions matter.

The same holds true for your Internet series. Clearly, you can't have a 90-second main title for a show whose episodes will only run three to five minutes. But this doesn't mean you can't create something short but memorable, a signature beginning that will lure the audience and serve as a quick visual and audio reminder of the tone, flavor and main thrust of your show. In short, what you want to create is a form of what marketing people call branding for your show — a quick hit that brings a smile to the viewer's face and makes him say *Oh yeah, I like that show.*

Your main title can also help "set the table" for your series and each individual episode. It can establish the tone of your show, introduce the main character, or even fill in the backstory so people who may not have seen the pilot can still understand and enjoy future episodes. Classic examples of this "tell the story of the series in the main title" approach from network TV include *Gilligan's Island* and, more recently and compactly, *My Name Is Earl.* A good prototype of this technique in a web series is the main title for *Mommy XXX* on Crackle. Though the name of the series suggests a great deal about its content, the main title goes further and lets you know it's a comedy, not an actual triple-X-rated series about moms. Accompanied by intentionally hokey visuals and a music track right out of a 1950s family sitcom, the main title voice over is: "Hi, my name is Demi Delia. This is my daughter Brandi, and this is my son Craig. Welcome to my family. Oh, and by the way... I'm a porn star." Then there's more hokey music and little hearts on screen, reminiscent of the *I Love Lucy* main title. It runs just ten seconds, but manages to set the tone, premise, introduce the characters and basic situation, and is funny all by itself, which entices you to watch the show. That's a well-designed main title.

Surf the Net, check out the variety of main titles out there, and ask yourself *what would make a great main title for my show?* The thought and effort will be paid back tenfold by how much a good main title will enhance the viewer's enjoyment and connection with your show.

And while we're at it, let's not forget the **end credits** either. In the early 1990s, network television figured out that just running the end credits for a show over a black screen, or even over still frames from the episode, is a waste of airtime. Viewers tune out the second the content on screen stops being worth watching, and there's nothing compelling about watching a bunch of names and credits for the people who supplied the lights or the catering. TV networks could almost hear millions of remote controls turning off the set or switching to another channel the instant the end credits began, meaning millions of viewers weren't watching the next show or next commercial on that station. So the networks finally wised up and urged shows to run original material or humorous outtakes behind the credits.

The same principle holds true for web series. Just as first impressions matter, so do final impressions, so keep them entertained right to the very end. Think of your end credits as an opportunity to make your viewers' final thought be *I love that show. I've got to watch another episode... and tell my friends about it.*

My students' show *Red White & Blue* (available at Funny Or Die) is a good example of keeping the entertainment going right through to the last crew credit. Each episode took a different approach — some continuing the action from the show, some spoofing other TV shows. But in every case, they found a way to make the end credits entertaining.

● FOR TEACHERS…

The best piece of advice I can offer on postproduction instruction is this: if at all possible, make sure you have at least one experienced editor in your class population. This may mean asking the students who sign up what their skill set is before the semester begins, or on Day One, and doing a little recruiting if nobody raises their hand when you ask if there are any experienced editors in the group.

Editing is a craft and an art form that is similar to music — some students have a gift and passion for it, some don't. It requires far more than knowing how to work the software and hit the right buttons. It requires a sense of rhythm within each individual scene as well as within the piece as a whole. And it requires more than a little experience to be able to watch a scene, identify ways to re-edit to strengthen it, and have a feel for the dozens of techniques that editors employ to maximize the effectiveness and impact of a cut.

That said, you'll also need to involve the entire class during the screenings and discussions of each successive cut. I've found that what works best is to screen the cut without stopping or commenting, then ask for overall or "big picture" type notes; e.g., *we need to tighten the opening and get to the story quicker* or *it drags in the middle* or *we need more reaction shots, not just shots of the person talking.* After the students offer their "big picture" observations, you can add any of your own that they haven't covered. Then screen the cut by starting and stopping wherever anyone, including you, has something he wants to discuss or suggest.

Because my classroom is a seminar setup rather than an editing suite, my process is to merely convey the notes to the editor, then let him/her execute them and generate a new cut for the following class session. But I can also imagine value in conducting some sessions in an actual editing suite, where the students can see first-hand the different performance choices from the dailies, or how each individual editing choice can change and improve the moment and overall quality of the piece.

CHAPTER TWELVE
BUILDING ON THE PILOT — COMING UP WITH EPISODE IDEAS

A great pilot is a wonderful accomplishment. You've created a world and a set of characters and relationships that have a palpable reality. You've (hopefully) gotten an audience hooked and now they want more. When you show a pilot, you are making an implicit promise to your audience that there's plenty more where that came from. And (presumably) you had at least a half dozen ideas for future episodes come to mind when you developed the basic premise way back when and asked yourself *does this concept have legs?*

So does that mean you should just pick any one of those half-dozen story ideas you cooked up way back when and use it to start developing a script for Episode 2? Maybe. But maybe not. Before you make that decision, you should take a step back and take a fresh look at your pilot. After all, when you came up with that original set of ideas for future episodes, you were flying blind. You hadn't actually written the pilot script. You didn't have a cast, and you hadn't seen the whole thing on film, cut together and in final form.

In short, you've got a boatload of newer, more detailed information than you did when you were first dreaming the whole thing up, and this information must be taken into account in developing your series going forward.

Not only do you have new thoughts, but now would be a good time to get some feedback from others. Unlike when all you had was a rough cut, now you have a finished, polished pilot with a great main title, clean sound, music, and a dynamite ending. It's time to take your baby out for a spin and see how an audience responds to it. You may be surprised as to which parts of your show the audience relates to the most. Your favorite parts and characters may not be their favorites. They may absolutely love a character or dynamic that you thought was merely incidental and not your strongest asset. This sort of audience feedback is priceless. Despite the fact that you are the show's creator, listening to the audience is vital because they are the ultimate judges of the material in the marketplace.

Time and again, pilots are made with the intention of the series progressing in one direction, only to have the unpredictable alchemy of casting, world events, audience response and a hundred other factors push the show in a new, unexpected direction. In the pilot of *Happy Days*, The Fonz was a minor character who had all of six lines. But the audience instantly fell in love with that character, as portrayed by Henry Winkler, so The Fonz quickly went from background player to the star of the show. This, of course, meant that either new stories needed to be developed focusing on The Fonz, or that The Fonz needed to be given a more prominent role in any story previously considered for development.

Same thing for the current CBS comedy *The Big Bang Theory*. By its original design, Leonard, played by Johnny Galecki, is the central role. He's the one with the love interest in the girl across the hall, and Johnny Galecki's credit comes first in the beginning of the show. But those design and contractual decisions were made before the pilot was shot, before episodes aired and the audience was exposed to Jim Parsons, Galecki's costar who plays smug, obsessive-compulsive, hyper-intellectual, socially clueless Sheldon. Parsons, as Sheldon, consistently scored big with the audience. The more laughs he got, the more material the writers created for him, and the more the show tilted toward Sheldon, who had become, as they say in the TV biz, a "breakout" character.

Your series is a living organism; it evolves over time, changing, growing, adapting in a Darwinian fashion by emphasizing its strengths and reducing or eliminating its weaknesses. But unlike organisms which evolve without conscious effort, your series can only evolve and grow if you help it to do so. In television, growth must be engineered. From the pilot on, that is the constant job of the series creator — nurturing, adapting, expanding, deepening, and growing the series. The pilot, wonderful as it may be, is only the beginning, a newborn that can only reach its full potential with the help of parental guidance. You've whetted the audience's appetite; now you must fulfill their craving and give them more — not just another helping of the same dish, mind you, but something that gives them new flavors and textures. Think of it as your wedding day, a glorious and memorable celebration, but only Step One in a very long journey with twists and turns and unpredictable developments galore ahead.

Growing Your Series

There are a handful of basic ways in which a series can grow. In no particular order, they are:

- New characters.
- New relationships between existing characters.
- Changes in circumstances for one or more characters.
- Deeper exploration of aspects of your characters.
- Increased emphasis on one or more formerly minor characters.

Let's look at each of these, using the long-running network series *Cheers* as an example of each of these techniques. The *Cheers* pilot is considered masterful. It received an Emmy for Outstanding Writing in a Comedy Series. But for all its greatness, the series would have languished and disappeared quickly if the writers and producers merely delivered "same song, second verse" in each subsequent episode. Instead, they took the pilot and built on it, keeping the audience coming back for 272 more installments over eleven award-winning seasons. They consistently grew the series using all of the above techniques.

New characters. The series characters presented in the *Cheers* pilot are Sam, Diane, Coach, Carla and Norm. Cliff, though present in the pilot, was merely a guest star, not a series character as yet. Frasier was added in Season 3 as a new love interest for Diane. This was clearly a brilliantly conceived addition — adding an intellectual counterpoint to Sam's good-time skirt-chasing perspective. Not only did the character help to keep *Cheers* fresh and alive for another nine seasons, but Frasier was spun off into his own series which lasted another eleven seasons.

When Nicholas Colasanto, the actor who played Coach, died suddenly after Season 3, Woody was added. Also added along the way were Lilith (Frasier's post-Diane love interest and eventual wife) and Rebecca, brought into the series when Shelley Long opted out after Season 5. Each new character brought new dynamics to the series, and each new dynamic brought dozens of new stories and angles to explore.

New relationships. In the case of *Cheers*, evolving relationships were part of the core plan for the series from its conception. In the pilot, Sam and Diane meet for the first time. She's an intellectual snob and he's only looking for a good time, but the sexual tension is there from the moment Diane, alone in the bar for a moment, answers the house phone and takes a message for Sam, who implores her to cover for him in order to avoid speaking to the woman calling for him. As she hangs up, he inquires about the message:

```
                    SAM
        Well?


                    DIANE
        You're a magnificent pagan beast.


                    SAM
        Thanks. What was the message?
```

The pilot was merely the beginning of a long, twisting journey for Sam and Diane, and the series. They were antagonists with a smoldering sexual tension between them for the first season. Then they were lovers with diametrically opposed interests (other than sex) for Season 2. Then they broke up, but still had feelings for each other starting in Season 3. Each new permutation in the relationship gave the series a fresh angle to explore and new stories to tell based on this new set of circumstances and character dynamic. You see this all the time on TV, from *Full House* to *House*. The characters enter into new relationships, or end old ones to explore the possibilities of new ones. The reason for this is simple: new relationships equal new stories and new growth for the show.

Changes in circumstances for your characters. This is really a variation on the new relationship concept. On *Cheers*, the primary new circumstance came in tandem with Kirstie Alley's entrance onto the show as Rebecca. Sam was no longer the owner of the bar, but was now merely an employee of a large corporation and, more importantly, was now subservient and forced to answer to an attractive woman, Rebecca, his new boss. In her debut episode, Rebecca explains Sam's new situation to him using a baseball metaphor:

> REBECCA
> It's the bottom of the ninth, you've got
> two outs, two strikes, and no balls.

This line is not only a funny joke. It also promises a brand new set of stories and story angles that can now be exploited by the writers.

Family sitcoms have made hay for years by having the sweet, innocent pre-teen girl suddenly blossom into a young woman with an interest in the opposite sex, instantly generating anxiety and problems for mom and dad (and new story ideas for the writing staff!). On *Roseanne*, the title character and her husband Dan were constantly adapting to new job circumstances — sometimes employed, sometimes unemployed, sometimes working for themselves. Each new circumstance provided a new environment and set of character issues to be explored.

Deeper exploration of your characters. When we pitch and develop a pilot, we have a tendency to reduce the complex humans in the world we create to a one-line description. Sam is a womanizing recovering alcoholic. Diane is an uptight intellectual snob. Norm is an inveterate beer guzzler who spends more time at the bar than at home. But human beings — at least the interesting ones — are multidimensional creatures who often surprise us with new and undiscovered aspects of their personality. So, too, with effective series characters. Yes, of course Norm will make his entrance into the bar each week and sit on that stool sucking his beer until closing time. But the producers and writers were also smart enough to know that there is value (and story material) in taking a closer look at Norm and his inner life. What would happen if a woman suddenly pursued a sexual relationship with Norm? Would he succumb to temptation or would he be faithful to Vera, his unseen wife on the show? They did an entire episode based on this premise. In the end, Norm remained faithful to Vera, and in the process of exploring this deeper aspect of the character, the audience now had a deeper and stronger bond with the character of Norm. This is the great value of deeper character exploration — it not only gives you a premise for an episode, it enhances your audience's connection and devotion to the characters and, in turn, your series.

Increased emphasis on one or more formerly minor characters. We've already seen how this worked with The Fonz and *Happy Days*. And we've mentioned how know-it-all mailman Cliff Clavin went from amusing spice to part of the main entrée on *Cheers*. The point is that when you go looking for ways to grow and expand your series, you may already have the answer embedded in your pilot or other episodes. Do you have a minor character who the audience loves? Then maybe that character is ripe for increased emphasis, either as a recurring character or a new costar for your series. On the long-running ABC comedy *Family Matters*, the character of Steve Urkel was originally intended to be a one-shot guest in a single episode. Enter Jaleel White and his engagingly off-the-wall portrayal of the hapless nerd. By the end of the taping of this one episode, the audience spontaneously rose to its feet and chanted, "Ur-kel, Ur-kel, Ur-kel!" A series regular and star of the show was born.

Growing Your Characters

In a television series, the characters must be consistent from week to week, speaking and acting in the manner the audience has come to know and love. And yet, for a series to sustain interest over a long period of time, these same, consistent characters must also grow and change. How can these two seemingly contradictory things be accomplished simultaneously? That, in a nutshell, is one of the most important elements in the art of writing series television.

As the previous section indicates, the principle source of series growth is, essentially, character growth of one kind or another. But TV characters don't — in fact, *can't* — change the way that characters in a one-shot story, like a movie or a novel, can change. The reason for this is fairly simple — in a one-shot form, the story is over when the piece is over. But in series television, the story goes on, episode after episode. So the characters can only grow and change in incremental ways. And yet, to maintain audience interest, the characters and situation cannot be so static that the audience becomes bored, filled with a sense that they've seen it all exactly this way before and that the series has "run out of gas."

What's a writer to do?

One way to look at it might be that rather than shooting for wholesale character changes (as one might in a one-shot movie or novel), the TV writer maintains interest in his main characters by constantly throwing new and greater challenges at him. Take Sam Malone, the devoted skirt-chaser on *Cheers*. When Sam got together with Diane, he was not suddenly transformed into a monogamous boy scout, content to look no further than the woman he was with. He was still a womanizer — but now he was a womanizer in a committed relationship *trying* to stay loyal and faithful. This was a source of huge internal conflict for him, and page one of the writer's bible says conflict = story.

The same type of approach has been used on the Fox medical drama *House* to keep the title character fresh and the series alive and growing. Dr. Gregory House is an unsentimental medical genius who strives for the worst possible bedside manner, the least sympathetic attitude toward his interns and underlings, and who pops painkillers like candy, side effects and warnings of the dangers of addiction be damned. If House suddenly became a sober, nurturing mentor with a gentle bedside manner, the audience would abandon the show, stat. He wouldn't be the same character they've come to know and love. But the writers know that complete character inertia can be equally deadly to a show's health. So they've turned the heat up on House by presenting him with greater and greater challenges to his curmudgeonly demeanor. His formerly timid interns and underlings have gained the confidence to push back when House pushes their buttons. His addiction has begun to threaten his ability to work — and without work, House would go crazy. So again, these new challenges = conflict = new stories = sustained audience interest.

Learning From Each Episode You Shoot

Serendipity has been an essential component of many great discoveries. Decades ago, a Mrs. Wakefield, owner of the Toll House Inn, was making chocolate cookies but ran out of regular baker's chocolate, so she substituted broken pieces of semi-sweet chocolate, assuming they would melt and blend into the batter. They didn't melt and chocolate chip cookies were the result. Percy LeBaron Spencer of the Raytheon Company was walking past a radar tube and noticed that the candy bar in his pocket melted, leading to the invention of the microwave oven. And in 1992, Welsh scientists were testing a potential new heart drug and accidentally discovered Viagra.

The moral of the story: sometimes the wonderfully unexpected pops up all by itself. But the unexpected only becomes a discovery instead of an annoyance if you're paying attention. Mrs. Wakefield could have cursed her semi-sweet chocolate chunks for not melting and thrown the batch in the trash. Mr. Spencer might have pitched his candy bar and maybe his soiled trousers and vowed to be more careful around radar in the future. And the Welsh scientists (and, presumably, the volunteers who took what they assumed was a pill to help their heart only to discover the rise of the unintended side effect) might have perceived their new drug as an embarrassing failure rather than the boon to men's sexual health (and advertising on football games) that Viagra has become.

The law of unintended consequences and random discovery is as potent in television as it is in the kitchen and the laboratory. But you must pay close attention, take note when fate has knocked on your door, and do something to capitalize on your good fortune. If you write a part for a guest star, and the actor you cast hits a home run with the audience and they love him, for God's sake, don't just sit there and smile. Write that part and that actor into your next episode, even if you hadn't planned on it. If you suddenly discover that your main character is hilarious when he goes off on a long-winded political tangent, write another one for him and see if it works again. Each and every episode should be viewed as a learning opportunity, another pilot, if you will; it's another chance to add to your series.

In fact, I'll go a step further and make the case that you can't merely wait for luck to show up on its own. You have to go looking for it. For your series to grow, you need to constantly experiment with new combinations of characters and situations and pay attention to the results.

The corollary to this approach, naturally, is knowing when the characters and situations that have been working well for your series have crossed over that fine line between "tried and true" and "Oh God how many times are they gonna do *that bit* on this show." Unfortunately, there is no hard and fast rule or battery-powered measuring device that can tell you when a joke or character dynamic has become stale. But if you find yourself getting a bit weary writing the same type of thing over and over, there's a good chance the audience is feeling the same way about watching it *ad nauseum*. However wonderful that joke or character trait might have been in its day, it's time to let it move on to the great TV afterlife. Thank it for its service, wish it well, but say goodbye. Breaking up is hard to do, but you're a creative person and will find something new to take its place.

How Many Episodes Do I Need Before I Can Post My Series?

Good question — and like all really good questions, there is no one absolute answer, just more questions. How many episodes are you planning to shoot overall? Six? Sixty? If it's six, you might want to wait until you've got them all ready to go before you post. But if it's sixty, it would be insane to wait that long.

Other questions include:

- How long will it take you to write, shoot and edit more episodes?
- Are your cast and crew going to bail on you if you don't start posting soon?
- Are you hoping to use the episodes to attract investors or other participants?

Uncertainty aside, let me offer some possible answers to the question at hand. For starters, I'd say that you'd be wise to post more than just the pilot — two or three episodes at a minimum. My reasoning is that you want to get the audience more than a little hooked. If they watch the pilot and can't see Episode 2 for another month, there's a good chance they'll forget all about your pilot and never get around to looking for Episode 2 when you do post it. If, however, they've seen the pilot and two more episodes, and they like what they've seen, the chances that they'll come looking for more in a month have gone up considerably. This isn't scientific, but I'd venture a guess that the odds of three episodes remaining close to the surface in a viewer's memory bank are about twenty times greater than if he'd only seen a single episode, the pilot. Again, not scientific, but ask yourself the difference in commitment you have between a show you've seen once and a show you've seen and enjoyed multiple times.

So three episodes is a good ballpark estimate on when to start posting. It's enough to get the audience fully engaged, but not so many that it'll take another year before you can post the next batch of fresh episodes. Even if, due to the nature of your series, you manage to crank out six episodes in a week, it may well be to your strategic advantage to post three, and then post the next three in a week or two. That way you can constantly be offering your audience something new and fresh, rather than giving them six all at once, having them gobble them up, then forget all about you before you post the new stuff a month later.

● FOR TEACHERS...

In my experience, coming up with story ideas for subsequent episodes is one of the most challenging assignments for students. I believe this is because the vast majority of students have never been asked to devise more than one story about the same set of characters using the same premise. Because of this lack of experience, plan on being a bit more "hands on" in your guidance than you normally are.

First off, require them to not only come in prepared to pitch story ideas for subsequent episodes, but to explain how their idea will help the series and/or characters grow. It may even be valuable to have a class session where you and the students brainstorm and pitch not stories but potential directions and avenues of growth for the characters and premise. This sort of broad conceptualizing will ground the students' thinking in the deeper purpose of adding to the palette of the series rather than merely devising some trivial incident around which to base an episode that may not contribute any new dimension to the show.

It may also be useful to ask them to watch a successful pilot and the next two first-season episodes of that series, and to then write a brief analysis of how Episodes 2 and 3 helped to grow either the series premise or characters.

If, despite all of your efforts, you find that the students' story pitches are still less than stellar, feel free to jump in yourself, specify a type of series or character growth you'd like to see in Episode 2 or 3, and ask them to pitch new story ideas in the next class session based on these tighter guidelines.

CHAPTER EIGHT
POSTING YOUR SHOW ON THE INTERNET

In the movie *Field of Dreams*, a mysterious Voice in the Sky insistently tells Iowa farmer Kevin Costner that *If you build it, they will come.* Being a trusting, New Age sort of guy who attended UC Berkeley in the '60s and believes in peace, love, granola, and the infinite possibilities of the universe, Kevin decides this Voice might be onto something groovy, so he plows under his crops and builds a baseball field. Lo and behold, the universe responds by delivering thousands of baseball fans to Kevin's farm, presumably bringing him fame and fortune, repairing his relationship with his dead father, and solving every other problem in Kevin's life.

Apparently, that's just how the universe rolls: *If you build it, they will come.*

I too am a UC Berkeley alum, a big fan of peace, love and granola, and think the universe is freaking awesome — my favorite place to live. But *If you build it, they will come*, while it may be great advice for spiritually inclined, baseball-loving corn farmers, is a terrible plan of attack for the creator of an Internet TV series. Building it is not nearly enough. If you want to fill the bleachers with fans of your show, you're going to have to be a very non-'60s, business-oriented, 21st century type and market that sucker 'til it screams. You need to be loud, proud, and pimp your show every which way you can. And why not? You've made a great show, now it's time to let as many people as possible know about it and then tell ten friends who have ten other friends who have still ten more friends that they should watch your show.

You've already been Kevin Costner; you've already built it. Well done. Bravo. Far out, man. Take a bow. But now it's time to be the Voice in the Sky and tell everyone you can to point, click and watch your great new show. Your new, Internet-age mantra should be *If you SELL IT, they will come.*

How do you sell or market your video? By using the tools of the medium you're working in: the Internet. These tools include social networking sites like Facebook and MySpace, and finding ways to maximize the number of ways your video pops up on search engines like Google and Bing. But before we get to all that, let's start with the single most popular destination for fans of Internet videos: YouTube.

YouTube

Unless you're a multibillion-dollar media conglomerate with its own dedicated website that already receives millions of unique hits per month, the first place you should post and market your Internet TV show is YouTube. It's simple, free, provides high-quality technology to store and stream your work, attracts a huge, worldwide audience of video fans each and every day, can be linked or embedded into dozens of other sites. Best of all, YouTube has a built-in system to help you market your work. The system is known as **tags**.

Tags are keywords that are used to help identify the content and other relevant characteristics of your video. Whenever you upload a video to YouTube, you have the opportunity to enter tags that will help users who might enjoy a show like yours find their way to it. Tags help bring viewers to your show, even if they aren't specifically looking for it, but have expressed an interest in one of the subjects you have entered as a tag.

For example, let's say you've created a web comedy called *Roommates From Hell*. Obviously, your friends and family who go to YouTube and enter *Roommates From Hell* in the search box will find it. But even if you have a thousand Facebook friends and come from a very large Catholic family, your network of personal contacts is but a tiny fraction of your potential worldwide audience. To reach this larger audience — and on YouTube, we're talking about millions of potential viewers — you need to be thorough and creative about the tags you attach to your show. On *Roommates From Hell*, these tags might include:

- Comedy
- Bad roommates
- Dorm life
- College life
- Apartment life
- Pet alligators
- Nose picking

You should also include the names of your cast as tags. After all, they all have friends and family and Facebook buddies who may know there's a video with their friend in it but can't remember the name of the show or what it was about. Also, your cast members may appear in dozens of other videos, and the people watching those other videos may take note of the actor or actress and want to check out their other work.

Right about now, some of you may be thinking *Hey, what if I slapped a phony tag on my series, one that has nothing to do with my show but will get millions of hits... you know, something like "porn" or "Jessica Biel nude" or "Michael Jackson"? Wouldn't that be a great idea?* NO, IT WOULD NOT BE A GREAT IDEA! Why not? Because while it might bring traffic to your video for an hour or two, that traffic is quickly going to become angry and disappointed traffic, traffic that will complain to YouTube who will, in turn, pull your video.

Coming up with legitimate creative tags for your work as a means of expanding the universe of potential viewers is a worthy goal. Being intentionally deceptive or misleading with your tags is not only pointless, it's self-destructive. Don't do it.

Beyond YouTube

While YouTube is the dominant brand name for video hosting (just as Kleenex is for tissues and Levi's is for denim jeans) it is far from the only place you can or should post your web series. If you made ketchup, you wouldn't sell it only at one supermarket chain, even if that chain was huge like Kroger. What about the people who shop at Safeway, or Walmart, or Whole Foods? Wouldn't you want to reach them, too? Of course you would. You'd want to have your product available at every possible retail consumption point that made sense for you and your business plan. And if your product had special features, you'd want to make sure you displayed it at the outlets that best fit those special characteristics. For instance, if your ketchup was organic or health food oriented, you'd probably want to display it at a market that attracted health-minded shoppers, say a place like Whole Foods. Or if you made not ketchup, but salsa, you'd probably want to display it not only at mainstream chains like Kroger and Safeway, but at supermarkets that catered to Spanish-speaking and Latin American clientele.

As I mentioned in Chapter One, there are dozens of sites beyond YouTube to choose from, each with its own pros and cons depending on the specific traits and needs of your project. For instance, if your series is shot in HD or requires high-resolution support, you may want to consider posting it on Vimeo HD, Dailymotion, or HD Share. Other factors to take into consideration when choosing a host site are limitations on video length and limitations on uploading time. Many sites have ceilings on these elements, such as no video longer than ten minutes, or maximum upload time of one hour. If your project is longer than YouTube allows, or your upload time exceeds a site's limits, you may need to look elsewhere to find the host site that fits your needs.

Even if your project is short and requires only ordinary resolution support, it behooves you to consider the full spectrum of sites available to you. Stock your product everywhere and anywhere it might attract viewers. Unlike the business world where Kroger or Safeway may not take your product if you also supply it to the competition, most video sites are nonexclusive. They place no restrictions on the number of host sites where you can post your work.

The only circumstance under which you should consider restricting the number of sites where you post your work is if you feel the cumulative number of viewers has to hit a certain threshold in order for you to split ad revenue with the site host. If, for instance, a host site will split ad revenue with you once your video receives a minimum of 40,000 unique viewers, and you think you may attract 60,000 total viewers, it makes little sense to post your work twelve different places and get 5,000 viewers here, 6,000 someplace else, etc. But if your overall objective isn't ad revenue, then cast the net as wide as possible. You've got nothing to lose.

Publicizing And Marketing Your Series

Just throwing your web series up on YouTube and hoping that people find it on their own makes about as much sense as singing in your shower with the window cracked open and hoping a record producer drives by, hears you, and signs you to a multimillion-dollar contract. Not going to happen.

The only way creative work gets discovered is if the creator — perhaps with the help of some partners — puts as much work into publicizing and marketing his work as he put into creating it. For your creative efforts to attract an audience, the audience has to know the show exists, be drawn to watch it, and know where to find it.

Start with the obvious: your list of personal contacts. Send an email to everyone in your address book asking them to check out your show. Even better, include a link to your video on YouTube so all they have to do is click and watch, right then, while the idea is fresh in their mind. Do the same on Facebook and any other social networking site you belong to: post a notice about your great new show and include a link to it. In fact, post notices several times, perhaps every other day for a week or two. Some people check Facebook all the time; others only sporadically. You want to reach as many of your contacts as possible. Also, people's lives are busy. They may not have time to click through and watch your video when they read your announcement on a Monday, but might have time on Wednesday or Saturday afternoon.

Okay, that's Step 1 — direct solicitation to the people you already know. Good start — but don't stop there. What about all the people your contacts know beyond your own circle? Maybe you know two or three hundred people. But collectively each of them may know two hundred people. If you could widen the net by having each of your 200 contacts reach out to their 200 contacts — well, you've just expanded your outreach from 200 potential viewers to 40,000 potential viewers. That's how viral video happens: through the exponential power of a hundred people each telling a hundred others about a video they liked and then, in turn, each of them telling another hundred people about a video, and so on and so on until the audience is magically multiplied from hundreds to hundreds of thousands or perhaps even millions.

I don't mean to suggest that by sending out a quick email and one Facebook posting you will instantaneously have a loyal audience of millions for your work. There will, of course, be attrition along the way. Not all 200 of your contacts will watch your video, or like it, or serve as volunteer PR flacks for you by urging all of their contacts to watch your show. But you'll get a hell of a lot more viewers by enthusiastically and aggressively touting your show than by sitting on your hands and hoping the world will somehow stumble upon your work.

Are there any other large groups you belong to? Your church, perhaps, or some online hobby group like acoustic guitar players or model airplane enthusiasts? If so, and if they have an online forum or newsletter, then by all means post your link and promo blurb there as well.

It's even worth considering making a flyer about your show, with the YouTube link, and passing it out in front of your local supermarket, coffee house, or even dropping it in the neighbors' mailboxes. What have you got to lose? If you don't ask, you don't get. If you do... well, who knows? Even a dozen new viewers could eventually multiply into hundreds of loyal new fans when they tell their friends who also watch your show, like it, and pass the word along.

Finally, it's important to be as disciplined and professional about publicity and marketing as it was during the writing and producing of your series. Just as with your story and script, your marketing and publicity plan should be written down, in black and white, rather than just "kept in your head." When you rely on memory or whatever pops into your brain and happens to stick, it's a recipe for sloppiness, forgetfulness, and less than adequate follow-through. If, however, you write down exactly how you plan to market your series — a bullet-point list is a good way to go — then you not only eliminate the chance of forgetting things, you increase the chance that missing pieces of the plan will become evident to you. You can also share your marketing and publicity plan with fellow videomakers or even marketing people you might know who may have further suggestions or improvements to offer. By all means, if you know someone who is a marketing expert, take advantage of this contact and her expertise. Show her your plan and ask what she thinks. A simple suggestion from her could mean thousands more viewers for you.

Festivals And Contests

For the past several decades, the hundreds of film festivals held all over the world have been a tried and true method for independent filmmakers to have their work seen and discovered by film fans and industry professionals alike. Festival exposure — especially for those films that won awards at the festival — often led to wider distribution, sometimes by a major film studio. This distribution, in turn, led to larger audiences for these award-winning festival films and served as a jump-start for the professional careers of the filmmakers.

In recent years, independent TV festivals have sprung up, hoping to provide the same exposure and advancement opportunities for independent TV artists. These festivals almost always include categories for web TV projects, and the projects that are nominated for prizes are commonly scouted by major web video sites and other producers looking for the next hot show. So by all means, you should research the festival scene (changing and growing by the minute) and submit your pilot to any and all festivals that seem appropriate. Two of the more well-known festivals as of this writing are the New York Television Festival (*nytvf.com*) and the Independent Television Festival (*itvf.org*).

Should You Create Your Own Website?

In most cases, you and your show are better served by posting it on YouTube and other established video hosting sites. They have established audiences of devoted video fans, sophisticated search engines designed to help prospective viewers find your show, and they have an experienced tech staff dedicated to handling all technical issues 24/7/365 at no charge or expense to you. Unlike trying to decide whether to own your own car or rely on public transportation, this would be more like deciding between owning, maintaining and paying for your own car versus having someone drive you wherever you want to go, whenever you want to go, in a really nice car... for free. It's a no-brainer. There's absolutely no reason for you to go to the expense and trouble of creating, maintaining, and promoting your own website dedicated to just your little Internet TV series. Unless...

Well, there are several circumstances where it might make sense to have your own dedicated website. For instance, if your show is interactive, or solicits viewer suggestions for where the story might go next, then you would need to create a website for the series that could also handle that sort of regular communication process. Or if your series aspires to have a social networking aspect to it (a la *quarterlife* or *showbizzle*), then obviously you would need to create a site that accommodated both video hosting and the infrastructure to serve the desired social networking functions. Finally, if your series had any unusual technical requirements that aren't available on one of the existing video hosting sites — extreme high-resolution needs, say, or specific animation software — then you'd need to build a site with the required technical specs in order to fully serve your series.

But in 99.999% of cases, putting time, money and aggravation into building a site merely to exhibit your short-form Internet series is unnecessary and unwise. Point, click, upload, sit back, relax, and let YouTube do the driving while you put all your time, money and effort into creating more episodes or your next series.

● FOR TEACHERS...

The natural place to begin is by demonstrating how to upload a video to YouTube, with particular emphasis on maximizing potential viewer outreach by being thoughtful and creative when assigning tags. Next, take an online tour of the various sites with the students to give them a sense of which ones have special features such as high-resolution capability, longer running time or larger total file size limits, etc.

When it comes to social networking and its utility as a marketing and publicity tool, some of your students may actually be able to teach you (and the rest of the class) a thing or two. In addition to your own presentation, it's definitely worth going around the room and asking the students to share creative ways they or their friends have used Facebook, Twitter, or other technologies to network and publicize their work and accomplishments. Social networking is a world that is growing explosively and changing by the minute, and students are frequently among the early adopters on the cutting edge of this revolution.

This is also a topic where inviting a guest speaker — someone whose expertise is marketing and publicity — can make great sense. Most likely you are a filmmaker, not a marketing person. But just like your students, you must embrace the reality that today's film auteur must also be a film entrepreneur. You can model for the students the notion of reaching out to other experts by inviting them to visit your classroom.

CHAPTER FOURTEEN
INTERVIEWS WITH CREATORS

The people I've interviewed come from a variety of backgrounds. Some have extensive resumes of successful feature films and mainstream television series. Others have had success as actors and are looking to expand their creative endeavors by writing, producing, directing, or all three. And some are recent film school grads looking for a way to break into the biz. But all have one thing in common: they have created short-form series content for the Internet.

The projects themselves vary greatly as well. Some had the advantage of significant financial backing from venture capitalists. Some were made with pocket change.

But all of these creators have valuable experiences and insights to share and have been generous and forthcoming in doing so. I urge you to read the interviews and learn from them — and to pay back the favor by going online and checking out their work.

In addition to the interviews in this book, you can also find additional ones in both print and podcast form at my website: *bytesized.tv*.

Read, learn — and enjoy!

JERRY ZUCKER

Comedy pro returns to his roots

Jerry Zucker began his career at the Kentucky Fried Theater, where along with his partners Jim Abrahams and brother David Zucker, he honed his comedy chops writing and performing skits in front of a live audience. From there he went on to write, produce and/or direct (sometimes with his partners, sometimes not) the feature films *Airplane!*, *Ruthless People*, *Rat Race*, *Ghost*, and the *Naked Gun* series of films, among others. In 2007 he created National Banana, an Internet comedy site that in many ways was a return to his earliest work — short comedy sketches. Though the site itself is no longer running, the content created for it is still available on YouTube.

Zucker is a master of broad comedy — meaning comedy with broad audience appeal — and generously shares his insights on the emerging world of short-form content on the Internet.

BROWN: After working in feature films for so long, what made you decide to create for the Internet?

ZUCKER: I think I got a little tired of the long process of getting features made. I had friends who said, "You should do television. It's so instant, so fast" — but it's a long road to get a show on the air in television too. Then someone came to me with this opportunity to create product for the Internet and it just sounded like fun. It started like it was going to be a hobby or part-time thing. And then all of a sudden, we got more backing and offices and employees and it was like, "Uh-oh." We were a company.

BROWN: Expectations.

ZUCKER: I didn't have a lot of expectations, but I found it fun. You could do anything. We did whatever we wanted. I didn't have to get permission from a studio for anything. Sometimes we saw something on the news and did a bit on it that night or the next day and got it up within a couple of days. I found it a breath of fresh air because I was writing, directing, producing, and doing all these things without having to go through a long development process.

BROWN: In many ways National Banana reminded me of your roots in Kentucky Fried Theater, where you and your partners had a sketch comedy act for the stage.

ZUCKER: It very much reminded me of that and I loved that — back to my roots. I loved the energy. And it was the Wild Wild West. Nobody knew what it was going to become and where it was going to go, and that was always exciting.

BROWN: In many ways you also blazed the trail for Internet comedy with your feature film *Airplane!*, where the end credits aren't just an obligatory list of names but contain entertainment value as well — things like "Best Boy: Joe Smith, Worst Boy: Adolf Hitler." I always tell my students that in Internet video, every second counts, even the credits, so make them entertaining. So maybe you were thirty years ahead of the time.

ZUCKER: Yeah. Who knows?

BROWN: How many series did you create for National Banana? It was a mix of series and one-shot sketches.

ZUCKER: My original vision was to have a multipurpose comedy playground, a place where there were some series, some stand-alone video bits, but also an interactive component and different channels with things you could poke around on and explore — almost like comedy dating. I also envisioned embedded sponsorships and ads where we'd shoot something on green screen, and so in the background you could put whatever you wanted. I saw all kinds of possibilities, but quickly realized how much time and money would be needed to build something that complex.

BROWN: Well, one of the things that I'm beginning to piece together in talking to different people who are doing work for the Internet is that the huge players like Sony have such deep pockets that they can invest a fortune in the future of Internet TV and just wait it out. And then on the other side of the spectrum, kids just getting out of school working on a shoestring can survive because they have no overhead. But people like yourself — who have significant backing but not the unlimited deep pockets of a Sony — have found it tough to generate enough revenue quickly enough to keep the venture going.

ZUCKER: You want to do more than just throw a bunch of videos up there. You want to do text to voice, and interactive, and multiple channels. But each component is time consuming and expensive. And so here's a question that I don't even know the answer to: If I had the money to put all that stuff up, would it have eventually brought in enough revenue to make a profit? I don't know. It's kind of a chicken and egg question: which comes first, investing in technology and content or building a revenue stream?

BROWN: Well, no one knows right now...

ZUCKER: No one knows. But I have this feeling that if you put the same time and energy and money and commitment into building a website that it takes to build a cable network, and the site is consistently fresh and entertaining, then I think that could work and become a sustainable business model.

BROWN: Let's change gears here to the creative because that's really what you're most interested in. What did the Web allow you to do that you couldn't do in studio features or network television?

ZUCKER: Well, first of all, there was no ratings board. I don't think a network would have let us do "Sands of Passion," our "Al Qaeda Soap Opera." Certainly that's one thing. The other is you don't need fancy equipment or as big an operation. So if you screw up it's not a big deal. You can experiment. I would look at a bunch of bits that we shot and say, "You know, this just isn't funny." So we wouldn't post it. You can't do that with a high-budget television show or a movie.

BROWN: Was that freedom to make mistakes liberating?

ZUCKER: Absolutely.

BROWN: Well, it's interesting that Paramount, the studio that released *Airplane!*, just announced a similar "low cost" model that they're going to try in feature films — funding twenty movies each with a budget under a $100,000.

ZUCKER: We certainly have come to a point now with the advent of the Red Cam and 4K video that you can make a high-quality movie with relatively inexpensive equipment. But you still need a great script; that doesn't change. Look at *Paranormal Activity* [whose production costs were reportedly about $15,000] — a really interesting idea, really well marketed. It's an idea that works without production expense.

BROWN: And they only have to have a hit one out of twenty times and they can still make money.

ZUCKER: Yeah. On the other hand, $100,000 is still a substantial amount of money. I don't think the studio will just greenlight anything. You still need a good script.

BROWN: Do you think there is a business model to be had out there for short-form Internet video but we just haven't quite found it yet?

ZUCKER: I think the problem is that you need eyeballs, and so the real question is: can you do something on the Internet that brings in a lot of viewers on a consistent basis. It's about content, as it always is.

BROWN: I worked for a successful comedy writer and director in the early '80s and we were discussing the changing technology of the time and how it might affect the movie business and he said, "They can put them on cassettes, they can put them on disks, they still need the funny," and that's what he does and that's what you do.

ZUCKER: I think that's true and I think that our website really failed because it never got to be great. I mean, there was funny stuff on it but it never ever got to be a great mainstream site. I think it can be done and I think as soon as someone does get a great comedy channel on the Internet, the eyeballs will be there and the money will follow. Right now most of the sites just aggregate content. Everybody thought more was better and that if they had thousands of video bits up, they'd be successful. But nobody wants to hunt through tons of video bits to hopefully find one or two good ones.

BROWN: The audience wants some assurance of a level of quality.

ZUCKER: Look at the highest level of show, like *Seinfeld*, which just delivered quality every week. You couldn't wait to get there to watch the next *Seinfeld*. That's not going to happen with aggregating a whole bunch of little bits from all over the place.

BROWN: Maybe a good print equivalent would be The Onion.

ZUCKER: Well, The Onion really is one of the few comedy products that has worked on the Internet, and The Onion is very funny and totally a consistent experience every time you log on. The problem I think with The Onion is that they've self-limited the site to news satire. Everything has to be in the form of a news report. They're brilliant at it, and it's wonderful, but it's limited.

BROWN: So, what you'd like to see is a broad-based Internet comedy channel where you go for a variety of comedy.

ZUCKER: Yes, exactly. But instead of a kind of Comedy Central on cable, with a different show every half hour, it has to be all these different places you can go to find not just shows but unexpected little comedy treats, surprises, constant variety — but all of a solid level of quality.

BROWN: Are you interested in working in the Internet realm in the future?

ZUCKER: I loved it — especially the immediacy and the creative freedom. I'm working on some feature projects now, one that we're editing, a couple that I hope to be directing, which I really enjoy. But I'd do Internet again in a second if I thought there was a way to do it right. It was fun.

BROWN: Great. Well, we'll look forward to your next Internet comedy.

ZUCKER: Great, but don't hold your breath.

CHRISTINE LAKIN

Child actor all grown up and producing now, too

Christine Lakin began her acting career at the tender age of 7 as the youngest member of the Atlanta Workshop Players. She then starred in dozens of national and regional commercials for top ad agencies before landing her debut film role at age 11 in the TNT Civil War drama *The Rose And The Jackal*. Shortly thereafter she landed the role of "Al" Lambert on the hit ABC sitcom

Step By Step (where the author of this book served as head writer and executive producer for six years.) After the series ended and she entered adulthood, Christine continued to act extensively in theatre, independent films, and in guest appearances on TV including *CSI*, *3rd Rock From The Sun*, and *Veronica Mars*.

Can a child star make the transition to becoming a working adult actor? Christine takes a humorous look at exactly that question in her web series *Lovin' Lakin*, where she not only stars, but also serves as writer, producer and creator.

BROWN: Tell us about *Lovin' Lakin*: where did the idea come from, what is the premise, and how did you decide to do it?

LAKIN: *Lovin' Lakin* is a web series that I created. It's a spoof of my real life, a mockumentary. It follows the life of "Christine Lakin" — a fictional and much dumber version of me — who used to be on the TV show *Step By Step*, and she is documenting her comeback to Hollywood as a service to others who might want to follow in her footsteps.

BROWN: *Step By Step* happened when you were a child actor...

LAKIN: Right.

BROWN: And so this comeback is as an adult now?

LAKIN: Exactly. I was taking this writing class and my friend Dave Mahanes came to me and said, "Hey, I've got this documentary company, we've got a bunch of equipment. Wouldn't it be fun to work on something together?" I said, "Well it's funny you say that, I've got this idea, but I haven't fleshed it out." So we sat there and talked for about an hour and said, "Is this a reality show?" and I said, "No, not a reality show, but something that's a spoof of my real life so I can make fun of myself and there's nothing I like to do more than make fun of myself." So we worked on how we would do it and then I wrote a bunch of outlines. I thought that I would just call some of my actor friends and kind of improvise the outlines while the camera was rolling...

BROWN: Knock it out real fast.

LAKIN: Right — then put it on YouTube to see what happened. But I made dinner one night with my boyfriend [writer/director Andy Fickman], and I had a couple glasses of wine and started pitching him the idea of the show, and he starts to laugh and says, "This is really funny, that's a great idea, why don't you guys come in and talk to Betsy and I about it?" Betsy Sullenger is his production partner in Oops Doughnuts.

BROWN: Oops Doughnuts?

LAKIN: Oops Doughnuts.

BROWN: You say that like it's a perfectly normal name for a production company.

LAKIN: Oops Doughnuts is Andy's company at Disney.

BROWN: I hate to get off the track of the *Lovin' Lakin* show, but where did the name Oops Doughnuts come from?

LAKIN: Andy's son, when he was four, walked around the house for no reason whatsoever saying, "Oops Doughnuts." And Andy always thought it was such a funny *non sequitur* that it would be a great name for a company.

BROWN: OK. Mystery solved. So you went to Andy's production development people...

LAKIN: And we sat down and just kind of said, "Hey, so this is our idea. We have these outlines; this is kind of what we're thinking about doing." I was assuming that they were just going to give us some advice, and they both said, "Well, we think it's a great idea if you guys could show us some scripts, we might be interested in producing this." And I casually said, "Yeah, sure, no problem." Then I went home and realized I had absolutely no idea how to actually put my ideas into script form. So I called my writer friend Ross Patterson and said, "I have these outlines, can you help me turn them into scripts?" He read them and said, "Lakin, this is really funny, you have more than enough material here for a web series." So we began this really great dialog over the next three months where he would take a pass at writing an episode, I would re-tweak, then I started writing some of my own episodes off some of the ideas I had. And then I would send them to him to get his feedback and then he would tweak them.

BROWN: How many episode scripts did that yield?

LAKIN: Ten episodes. I showed them to Andy and Betsy, got their notes. We did a little more revision and they gave us a very small amount of money to go out and actually make this thing. We started filming in June 2009. I am very blessed because I have very funny friends, so we would do a couple takes that were scripted and then we'd say, "OK, let's just play and see what happens."

BROWN: So it's a mixture of scripted and improvised material?

LAKIN: Yeah. And the thing we started to find was the improvs were way funnier than the scripts. But we had so much material that it made editing difficult because the improvs went on tangents, and you need cut points.

BROWN: Right.

LAKIN: So while we were happy to have extra stuff we could show on our blog eventually, we realized we needed to overhaul the scripts and break them down into short, defined bits.

BROWN: To leave room for some of the improvisation.

LAKIN: To leave room for the improv and to also come up with firm cut points that we could use. You have to make sure that within the improv you still cover all the story points. So the moral of the story was that we started with outlines, expanded into scripts and ended up using the outlines plus parts of the scripts plus improv.

BROWN: But I assume that the script process still helped you refine the outlines?

LAKIN: Absolutely. Even when we "threw out the scripts" there were still lines that I loved that I would work into the improv...

BROWN: Or at least concepts that came out of the scriptwriting process that were embedded in your mind and then became part of the improv...

LAKIN: Totally.

BROWN: You managed to get some major celebrities to participate in your series. I certainly expected Patrick Duffy from your time on

Step By Step, but I didn't expect that you'd get Jamie Lee Curtis and Kristin Chenoweth and Kristen Bell to do the show.

LAKIN: Me either. I had a small part in Andy's film *You Again* and had met Jamie Lee Curtis. I figured I'd knock on her trailer door, ask if she'd be willing to do what I hoped might be a ten second bit for my web series. Not only did she say yes, she had this whole idea: "How about we do this, you go into my trailer, poke around in my things, then I'll come in and catch you." And what I got out of this impro-vised bit was an entire episode. She's absolutely genius in it and she's such a brilliant improvisational actress that we got a complete seven-minute episode with Jamie Lee Curtis.

BROWN: Talk about a great gift and a surprise.

LAKIN: A great gift and a surprise, and once Jamie Lee Curtis appeared in the show, Kristin Chenoweth was like, "Well sure, if Jamie did it I'll do it," and then it just snowballed and Kristen Bell agreed to do an episode. I'm very lucky.

BROWN: Having recognizable celebrities in your web series helps in two ways. It gives the series an authentic inside Hollywood feel, and it's also going to help you to market the show.

LAKIN: Some of the bits with celebrities will be made into ten-second viral teasers that we will put on Facebook and YouTube and will say "Want to see more? This is where you go."

BROWN: Are you going to post all the episodes at once, or make them available a few at a time, or week by week?

LAKIN: We'll probably go live first with an introduction to the series, two minutes of me talking to the camera, "Hello world, my name is Christine Lakin. You might remember me from *Step By Step*. I'm making my comeback to Hollywood and I'm doing this documentary so that I can help you, the viewer, understand what it takes to make a comeback to Hollywood." I'm just clearly an idiot, saying this is going to be bigger than any Michael Moore documentary or Ken Burns baseball thing. So that will go up probably for a few weeks to help build traffic, accompanied by photos, video clips, etc. Then we'll have a series launch date, do a premier somewhere here in Hollywood...

BROWN: And hope to get some press coverage.

LAKIN: Exactly. Then we will premier a different episode each week.

BROWN: That sounds like a solid plan.

LAKIN: We're also hoping that the web series might attract someone like a cable network interested in a longer version of the show.

BROWN: So the series could be grown into something more in a tradi-tional 30-minute or a 60-minute program length?

LAKIN: Absolutely.

BROWN: As TV and Internet video continue to evolve, do you see more mixing of genres — short-form series running right alongside tradi-tional half-hour and hour shows?

LAKIN: People watch TV in a completely different way now than they did ten years ago. People are now in front of their TVs, but also have their Blackberries by their side, their laptop in front of them. They're on Facebook watching *The Office* and looking at email — all at the same time. It's ridiculous, the amount of media you can consume at one time.

BROWN: Was part of the attraction of doing a web series the chance to grow some skills beyond your acting chops, skills like writing and producing?

LAKIN: Definitely.

BROWN: And now that you've done it, do you feel that those things have made you a better actor — given you an even larger set of tools to analyze scripts and character?

LAKIN: Absolutely. I look at a script differently now. As an actor you focus mostly on your character. Now I look at the whole picture: what's the tone of the show, the overall story, and the visual style. And I think that that's very helpful, I think it gives you a more grounded place to come from in making choices as an actor.

BROWN: Has this experience made you want to write and produce again — perhaps even beyond the web series realm?

LAKIN: Definitely. I just love the days where I get up and I know that I'm going to edit something that we filmed or I know that we're going to film something we wrote. I love working as an actor, but it's even more gratifying being involved with the entire process — taking a germ of an idea and developing it, putting together the production, and then following all the way through editing to completion.

BROWN: Cool. Anything else you want to tell us about *Lovin' Lakin*?

LAKIN: It makes me laugh, and I hope it catches on with an audience. But no matter what happens, I've learned a lot, had fun, and I'm really proud of it.

BROWN: It's a terrific show, so congratulations.

LAKIN: Thank you.

MARSHALL HERSKOVITZ

From network TV to the Internet

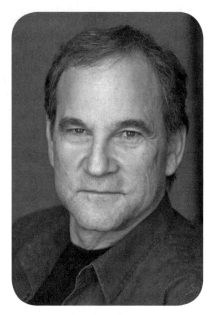

In conjunction with his long-time creative partner Edward Zwick, Marshall Herskovitz has written, produced and created some of the most acclaimed and timely dramas in television history. Their landmark series *thirtysomething* won a basketful of Emmys during its four-year run on ABC and is now part of the general public vocabulary. They then went on to produce *My So-Called Life,* the gold standard when it comes to cutting-edge teen dramas. Herskovitz and Zwick have proven time and again that they have a knack for tapping into the cultural zeitgeist and delivering compelling drama that explores that world. But could they translate this talent for thoughtful drama to the microseries world of the Internet, where an entire episode lasts only a few minutes? The top-notch quality of their pioneering Internet series *quarterlife* proves that the answer to that question is a resounding YES.

BROWN: You've had an enormously successful career in network television and feature films. What made you decide to create *quarterlife* and to work in the Internet television realm?

HERSKOVITZ: Well, I had actually become very frustrated with the business of television because decisions made by the FCC going back to 1995 allowed networks to own an unlimited amount of the programs that they aired. That started an inexorable process of the networks taking more and more control. And not just creative control, but business control. As a result you couldn't be independent. Basically, there was no such thing as an independent television producer anymore.

BROWN: It really was the death of independent production companies from people like yourself on up to huge companies like Stephen Cannell.

HERSKOVITZ: Right. So, Ed and I had been thinking a lot about the Internet for years. There was this notion going back even to 2002 that somebody was going to create a production and put it on the Internet and make $80 million directly through the Internet and you wouldn't need a studio, you wouldn't need a network, you wouldn't need any of the old distribution channels.

BROWN: A lot of authors had the same notion about books that they wouldn't need publishers or bookstores anymore.

HERSKOVITZ: Exactly. So, the point is we were influenced by that, and as I got deeper and deeper into it I began to feel that there could be an economic model with advertisers, where if you created the kind of programming that people could see on television, they would come to the Internet for it and if you did it at a very, very good price you could make money doing this. Now, it turned out that wasn't the case, but it was a valid argument and I decided I would give it a try. I had made a pilot for ABC called *Quarterlife*, but it wasn't the current show, it was a completely different story. And it didn't work terribly well. I actually offered to rewrite it for free for ABC because I wanted to get it right. So, I did, they passed on it and it was at that moment when I said, "Look, I have now created a story about the Internet, using the Internet as part of the series premise. This is the perfect show to do for the Internet." So we got it back from ABC and I made a pilot with my own money — plus I called in every favor I could. Once we had the pilot I tried to figure out what business this was, how we would go about making a series. In my case, I didn't want to just make a series. I wanted to create a social network. And so it was a more complicated enterprise than just trying to make content for the Internet.

BROWN: Did you have the social network in mind when you wrote the pilot?

HERSKOVITZ: No. When I finished writing the pilot is when it came to me that there was an underserved need. At that time Facebook was only open to students, it had not opened up to the general public yet. And we said to ourselves, if all these people leave Facebook when they graduate and they're out in the world, who's serving their needs? So I saw combining the show with the social network as a way to serve this audience of people in their 20s and early 30s trying to build their lives and careers.

BROWN: When you wrote the Internet version of *quarterlife*, did you take the pilot you had written for ABC and more or less use each 8- or 9-minute act as an Internet episode?

HERSKOVITZ: Yeah. We said, "Look, we've learned over 30 years how to make compelling act breaks so that people come back from the commercials, so this is just getting them to click on the next episode to find out what happens next." So, yes, we just took the six acts that had already been built into the one-hour script and turned it into six episodes.

BROWN: Most of what's on the Internet is broad comedy. But *quarterlife*, though it has a fair amount of comedy, does legitimate drama with legitimate character explanation and depth to it.

HERSKOVITZ: I was never convinced that you can't make anything longer than two minutes for the Internet just because that's what had worked so far. Even as we were doing *quarterlife*, more and more people were watching their favorite hour-long television shows on the Internet. So when people told us that having 8-minute episodes would doom us, I just didn't buy it. Last time I checked *quarterlife* was the most-viewed series of any series ever made for the Web, based on average views per episode. We have about 380,000 views per episode. *Lonelygirl15*, another series considered a big Internet success, had an average of 180,000 views per episode. Now it's possible that Joss Whedon's show [*Dr. Horrible's Sing-Along Blog*] did better, but he had a totally different distribution model that included iTunes.

BROWN: Right.

HERSKOVITZ: So I believe there's still a business to be discovered in Internet content, but nobody's going about it the right way yet. There's a chicken and egg problem here, which is that you cannot find enough money to do it right. But if I could raise the money to do it right, I'm convinced it can still work and I'm convinced that the magic number is a million views per episode. For me, the convergence between Internet and television takes place at a million viewers, about the size of the audience for *Mad Men* on cable.

BROWN: As another example, there's a site called Break.com that targets young men and gets about 750,000 hits a day — about the same number of viewers as Spike TV, a cable channel that targets young men.

HERSKOVITZ: I believe absolutely there's a way to get a million views per episode on the Internet now because even in the two years since we did *quarterlife*, marketing on the Internet has become so much more sophisticated.

BROWN: Absolutely.

HERSKOVITZ: So, if I could raise the money now, I would do a series on the Internet and I believe I could make money out of it, but I can't raise the money because it hasn't been done yet.

BROWN: Well, one thing that may help is increased use of the Internet by broadcast channels and major cables networks as a development laboratory. HBO now airs *Funny Or Die Presents*, a collection of skits from the Funny or Die website. And I just read that CBS is making a pilot based on a series of Internet and Twitter postings called *Shit My Dad Says*.

HERSKOVITZ: Oh, yeah, absolutely. It's got a huge following.

BROWN: I noticed you have two other shows listed on the *quarterlife* website.

HERSKOVITZ: Yes. We made two other pilots for web series — and neither of them by the way are dramatic, they're both documentary.

BROWN: There was one called *I Believe* about a person searching for faith. And the other one is sort of a behind-the-scenes show about the craft of filmmaking

HERSKOVITZ: Actually, that one [*Film School*] was just something we started to put together based on footage that we have. There's another pilot that we have not even put up on the site yet called *Unheard*, about indie music scenes around the country. And it's a wonderful little pilot. A lot of what I think helps make an Internet TV series work is when it has a clearly defined niche with an audience that will be devoted and loyal because the show is about something they're passionate about.

BROWN: Are you planning to produce or license more content for the Internet?

HERSKOVITZ: Not at the moment because I can't afford to. I used a lot of my own money and I lost a lot of money and until I can figure out a business model that doesn't entail me spending my own money, I'm constrained from doing any more.

BROWN: Do you think that because the networks see the development lab potential of the Internet that they might fund some of this so that it can reduce creator's financial risks?

HERSKOVITZ: Well, they tried that in various guises and many of them have already closed down. The Internet changes so quickly that I don't consider myself an expert anymore because I'm six months out of date. But what I saw six months ago was that scripted shows on the Internet were almost exclusively the domain of self-driven creators, and that it was not being funded by investors anymore. In other words, a year ago and two years ago, you had advertisers putting in a lot of money into producing Internet shows.

BROWN: Anheuser-Busch actually created an Internet channel: BudTV.com.

HERSKOVITZ: There was a lot of advertiser money being spent to create content. It was an experiment and it lasted about a year and then it dried up because they were not getting their money's worth out of it. So what I see mostly now is people doing their own thing with their own money for a dollar and a half and putting it up there. And, you know, I'm not sure that it's ever going to turn into something that's a business for the networks or for anybody else.

BROWN: Well, it may not, it may just be a way like short films for people to try to break in.

HERSKOVITZ: Exactly.

BROWN: So if you were talking to an aspiring filmmaker who wanted to make a web series, what kind of show should they make or what kind of advice would you give them?

HERSKOVITZ: You have to ask yourself a question if you're a young filmmaker, which is what are you actually aspiring to do? What is it you're trying to get out of this? Are you trying to be discovered as a filmmaker? Do you want to move on to a bigger canvas or do you want to find success on the Internet? There are different pathways there.

BROWN: Sure.

HERSKOVITZ: I would say if you are a filmmaker and you aspire to work in television or movies or the Internet then you've got to make something that's the best you know how to make. So don't limit yourself to comedy. You can make comedy, but it better be great. Do a drama, do something scary, do something that shows your talent as a filmmaker because the Internet is a remarkable way to put your work in front of people's eyes. When I came to California too many years ago to count, I had made a film and I couldn't get anybody to look at it. Now, you could put something out there and somebody is going to see it.

BROWN: The power of the Internet is amazing. I remember reading that the improvisational acting troupe The Groundlings here in LA went out in the alley behind their theater and taped some of their skits and got a deal to be on Sony's channel on Crackle.com. The skits were seen by more people in a few weeks on the Internet than if they sold out the house for 600 years.

HERSKOVITZ: You've got it — the Internet is an amazing outlet.

VALERIE SHEPHERD & MICHAEL ASHLEY

A way to break in

Valerie Shepherd and Michael Ashley are MFA Screenwriting graduates of the Dodge College of Film and Media Arts at Chapman University. Both are also skilled actors, with Valerie training for two years at the Lee Strasberg Theater Institute and Michael performing comedy sketches with the L.A. chapter of the Upright Citizens Brigade. They decided to combine their writing and acting talents with a healthy dose of self-mockery about their personal relationship and created their own web series called *Bad Love*.

BROWN: Valerie Shepherd and Michael Ashley are the creators and stars of the web series *Bad Love*, which can be seen on YouTube. Any place else?

ASHLEY: We have a website, too: *www.badlove.tv*

BROWN: Full disclosure, we all know each other from Chapman University, where I'm a professor and Michael and Valerie were graduate students in the MFA Screenwriting Program. Tell us about *Bad Love*, what's it about, how did you decide to do a series for the Internet?

ASHLEY: The show is about a couple like the ones portrayed on *Mad About You* or *Dharma & Greg* but with an irreverent and more current spin on it, like *It's Always Sunny In Philadelphia* or *Seinfeld*. Mike and Valerie are the kind of couple that loves each other madly, like those earlier TV shows, but they're awful to each other and they're awful to everyone around them.

SHEPHERD: The couple is much like Larry David's character on *Curb Your Enthusiasm*; he may be an awful person but you can't help but watch.

BROWN: It's a train wreck relationship.

SHEPHERD: Yes, yes. I think it literally came from our own experience, our own life.

BROWN: You're saying you have a bad relationship with each other?

ASHLEY: We're saying that we can be the couple that is *bad love* sometimes.

SHEPHERD: Yeah. Maybe, you know, make out inappropriately in public.

ASHLEY: Or crash a wedding and still try to sign the guest book.

SHEPHERD: I think at one point, we're at dinner and I was like, "We are so bad." If I saw us on the street I'd think, "Oh, my God. These people are so awful." And Michael said, "We're bad love," and we came up with the show.

ASHLEY: But we also do a lot of charity work.

BROWN: Nice. You step on puppies and then rehabilitate them?

ASHLEY: Right.

SHEPHERD: Of course.

BROWN: OK, that's good. How many episodes have you shot and how many more do you plan to shoot?

SHEPHERD: We shot five and they're edited, and we plan to shoot indefinitely. The good thing with webisodes... it's pretty cheap to produce them.

BROWN: How cheap? What's the budget per episode, or is there a budget?

ASHLEY: Well, I think that the budget for the most part is what we can contribute to it. We're lucky in the fact that we went to film school and we have friends that have technical skills. We have a director who is an actor too, and we have friends that have editing software and who were trained to be editors, and so we called in a lot of favors. We also have a friend that's a very good DP, who also teaches cinematography courses in L.A. Most of our costs are minor things like costume changes once in awhile, some food, and DV tapes.

SHEPHERD: But the answer is we are really relying on favors at this point.

BROWN: Do you shoot with available light or do you have a small lighting kit to augment things when you're doing the interiors?

SHEPHERD: Day shoots are sunlight and night shoots are whatever we have. At this point...

ASHLEY: Prayer. It's the prayer lighting system.

BROWN: Sure. And I don't think people watch web series for the production value. I think they watch them for the content.

ASHLEY: Right.

SHEPHERD: We're hoping.

ASHLEY: And as for sound, we got lucky because our director shoots weddings as part of his side job. He was able to get us lavelier mikes, which we used after the second episode which helped a lot.

SHEPHERD: I don't know if the people who own those mikes absolutely know that he — we kind of borrowed them.

ASHLEY: Because some of the biggest technical problems we've had are sound problems.

BROWN: Like the room we're in right now is pretty echoey.

SHEPHERD: And I'm sure you watched the episode where we filmed in this room...

BROWN: I was going to say, the sound was echoey in that scene. On the other hand, it sounds like what the room really sounds like, so it is not inappropriate because there is a certain... dare I use the word... *cinéma vérité* feel to the way it's shot.

SHEPHERD: Well, and I think when you're using the resources you have... it dictates the feel of the show anyway.

BROWN: How do you plan to promote and market the show? How do you get the audience to find the show?

SHEPHERD: To be honest there's no one path. We already have a Facebook page, a MySpace page, a Twitter account, a blog site, as well as our own personal website to market the show. And we're going to spend countless hours getting people to join our fan pages.

BROWN: I think you have to do that, otherwise you're just throwing the thing into the Grand Canyon and hoping it hits somebody in the head.

ASHLEY: What I think is that if you allow people to participate with your show and interact with the show — if they can blog and they can add commentary... and if they can become a fan and they can suggest you to other pages... it's different from TV in that it's more participatory, where they feel like, "Look, it's something cool I found. Let me share it with you." And so if we harness the social networking aspects of the Internet... we will have a chance to succeed in this new medium.

BROWN: What would you consider a successful audience population? A thousand people, five thousand people...

ASHLEY: We're going to think it's a thousand until we get to a thousand, then we're going to go for five thousand.

BROWN: Fair enough. You guys just graduated from film school not too long ago. Do you see working on Internet projects as a stepping stone to other things or as something that has value in and of itself, or both?

ASHLEY: I think it's both. We're both involved in other projects besides this. We have other jobs to pay the rent, we both write film scripts, and we also write TV specs for traditional network and cable shows.

BROWN: And this subject matter might not work in a feature film or in network television.

ASHLEY: Well, we want it to be picked up by network television, but since we don't have the connections where we can take this straight to the networks or cable, we're hoping this could be a launching pad to get us those kinds of contacts.

BROWN: That's a good plan. So what are the top three lessons you've learned about producing for the Net so far?

SHEPHERD: Less is more. Our webisodes so far run about five and a half minutes. But people on the Web have a very short attention span. In the future we're going to concentrate on telling a story in less time.

ASHLEY: I think also what we've learned from producing on our own is that you don't need a huge crew. We're basically the writers, the producers, the actors, the directors, and we will be marketing it ourselves. And I think what's really wonderful about this medium is that you can do all these things yourself and not have to outsource it or pay somebody to do it, and you have control over the creative aspects of it.

BROWN: What are some of your favorite web series, if you have any?

SHEPHERD: There's the group called Smosh.

BROWN: S-m-o-s-h?

SHEPHERD: Uh-hmm. It's not a series. It's more sketch comedy, but I think they literally just graduated from high school.

BROWN: One of the things I like about your series is, it's a comedy but it's not just a sketch comedy. It's a comedy that has more substance in the emotional dynamics of the show. Was that something you felt was important when you were creating the show?

SHEPHERD: There's a lot of sketch comedy out right now on the Web.

BROWN: It's unquestionably the dominant form out there.

SHEPHERD: So it was kind of a way to make a...

BROWN: To separate yourselves from it.

SHEPHERD: Yes, yes.

BROWN: What about your storyline? Do you have an overall arc for the relationship in mind or you're just going episode by episode so far and then thinking about your arc as you get deeper into the characters?

ASHLEY: I think that we began it with the idea that we're going to see what's going to happen the first season, and then I think what we'll probably do now that we're finished with the first season is go back and try to figure what we want to do for the upcoming season.

SHEPHERD: I think that's actually something that we discovered in writing the season; that we want an overall arc for our characters. Does this couple really love each other? Can we get more insight into them?

BROWN: The short attention span rule applies to not just individual episodes but to the growth of the series. You can't just do the same thing over and over again. You've got to progress the series and grow it somehow, or the audience loses patience with it.

SHEPHERD: Exactly.

ASHLEY: And I think a really helpful thing for me, at least, was to look at other shows, cable programs especially, because of the freedom those writers have to tell compelling and different stories. Some of the best writing in Hollywood is happening in television because you can do things in television you can't do in a 120-minute movie, like have an unsympathetic protagonist.

SHEPHERD: Being on the Internet instead of a network show allows us to push the envelope.

BROWN: Your main title is a good example of selling the show quickly in a short amount of time. It's very simple, just the two of you dancing together until he dips you and drops you on the ground.

SHEPHERD: And walks away.

ASHLEY: There's a lot of love in that.

BROWN: Last question for you. Where do you see Internet TV heading? Is it... I mean we all assume it's going to grow...

SHEPHERD: Yes.

BROWN: But how?

SHEPHERD: I believe that there will be a lot more crossover than there is now...

BROWN: Between broadcast television and the Internet?

SHEPHERD: Everybody's going to get their fingers in this... and it's going to grow and it's going to have more funding and bigger stars attached to these smaller projects. Plus the little, you know, the Emmy's for...

BROWN: The Streamy awards for online television?

SHEPHERD: Yes. I believe it will just grow from that and... I think it'll create more jobs.

BROWN: Well, it's the Wild West. Everybody's trying to figure it out right now, but the money players have not exhibited any more success than the people like yourselves who are doing it on a shoestring.

SHEPHERD: The big players do not know how to make money off of this medium yet, and that's why I think it is the creators who have the upper hand right now. I feel like when big money Hollywood figures it out, the people who have established themselves are going to have a good time, but it might soon become a mini Hollywood system, where then the doors close and it'll be harder to get in.

ASHLEY: We have a really good opportunity here to bypass the old system and to take advantage of this new technology. I think that we're very lucky to have this kind of chance in that we don't have to play by the studios' or the networks' traditional rules. I think you will find a lot of people beginning their careers in the way that an industry outsider like Andy Samberg did. He first got recognition on the Web that led to a gig on *Saturday Night Live*.

BROWN: It is a great incubation setting where you can inexpensively experiment, show your wares, have a chance to be discovered there, and have a chance to practice your craft as you're growing as artists.

CHARLES ROSIN

Internet 90210

Charles Rosin was the executive producer/showrunner for the first five seasons (144 episodes) of the original *Beverly Hills, 90210*. Under his creative stewardship the series received a People's Choice Award, two Golden Globe nominations, and numerous citations and awards for sensitive handling of contemporary issues. In addition to *90210*, Charles

wrote and produced numerous TV movies, pilots and series, including *St. Elsewhere*, *Remington Steele*, *Dawson's Creek*, and *South Of Nowhere*. As supervising producer of the acclaimed series *Northern Exposure* (for which he received an Emmy nomination), Charles wrote the episode "The Aurora Borealis," which *TV Guide* named as one of the 100 most memorable episodes in American television history. He created the Internet series *showbizzle* with his daughter Lindsey, a writer-producer-director in her own right.

BROWN: OK, I'm here with Chuck Rosin, who's the TV...

ROSIN: Professionally, can you call me Charles.

BROWN: We can.

ROSIN: Would make my wife happy.

BROWN: OK. I'm...

ROSIN: As a person, you call me Chuck.

BROWN: You got it.

ROSIN: But it's... but she likes Charles.

BROWN: OK. Starting over again...

ROSIN: R-O-S-I-N.

BROWN: I'm speaking with Charles Rosin. His TV credits include writing for shows like *St. Elsewhere, Remington Steele, Northern Exposure*, as well as serving as head writer and executive producer and show runner of *Beverly Hills 90210*, the original one. But we're here to be talking about his Internet project, *showbizzle.com*, which you created along with your daughter, Lindsey, yes?

ROSIN: Correct.

BROWN: And it's both a web series and a website?

ROSIN: It's two... two... two things in one — and you'd be surprised how difficult that is to grasp for a culture that's supposed to be so adept at multitasking.

BROWN: Describe it then.

ROSIN: *Showbizzle* is a digital showcase and destination website created for emerging talent, featuring a digital performance space away from the pressures of the marketplace. We have multiple channels. We have a community channel where we encourage people to upload their user videos. We also have something called "Inside the Bizzle" — interviews with industry professionals talking on a personal level about what it was like when they started out, how has the business changed.

BROWN: And within all that, there's also a web series.

ROSIN: Yes. At its core is the daily-weekly series called *showbizzle*, which centers on a fictitious blogger named Janey, a writer of screenplays, who's unseen, and who's an L.A. girl whose father is a famous movie producer. She hangs out at a coffeehouse and is only too happy to be interrupted from the arduous task of writing to hear about what's going on with her friends as they try to jumpstart their careers in Hollywood.

BROWN: And they have a variety of careers, actor, agent...

ROSIN: The series chronicles the hookups, breakups, screwups — all the things that people encounter in their first job experience. We started with ten actors each doing three monologues, and we shot that in January of 2008. So you would meet somebody like the character Melissa, who is thrilled that she's just been cast in the lead of a TV series, but they may want her to be bisexual. She then, in part two, realizes there's a lot of girl-on-girl stuff and she doesn't know how her priest and her parents are going to react, etc., etc., and in part three, she and her costar are moving in together up in Laurel Canyon. We did those 30 monologues and built a prototype website. But we got to July of 2008 and wanted to do a much bigger production... that's when we worked with all 43 actors. We ended up having 177 two-minute vignettes.

Though the original plan had been to post two to four new vignettes on the Web every day, making fresh material constantly available for, as Rosin describes it, "digital snacking," he and Lindsey quickly realized that the material they had might also be compelling as an interwoven ensemble. So they re-edited the footage, added off-screen dialogue and questions from the unseen Janey, and converted the two-minute monologues into multi-layered, interwoven stories that ran closer to fifteen minutes per episode.

BROWN: The stories are interwoven now and very cleverly so.

ROSIN: Thank you very much. The monologues are great for digital snacking. But some audiences prefer the longer, interwoven version, where each episode has a beginning, a middle, and an end.

BROWN: Well, you know, from watching the show, there are virtues to the video snacking as you call it, but it also works quite well in the longer format.

ROSIN: From a production standpoint, the monologue format was very clever and allowed us to keep our cost down. We shot the original 30 vignettes in two days. It was easy because the setup was the same.

After spending countless hours writing, shooting and editing these scripted monologues of fictional characters trying to break into the business, Charles and Lindsey had a revelation: there were also thousands of real stories out there about young people trying to break into the biz, and thousands of those young people are dying to share their stories. So they added a component to their site whereby members could submit a video of themselves telling their own story about showbizzle.

ROSIN: We realized members could do this because we'd given them a style they could emulate.

BROWN: They don't have to be actors. They just have to tell their story.

ROSIN: Exactly. Shows are organic things and they change over time... and change quickly in the digital sphere. Same goes for the business itself. When Disney announced they were selling *Lost* on iTunes, I said, if a show like *Lost*, which has an international following and is a huge hit on broadcast television, needs to be thinking about how they get ancillary revenue during its first run, this meant the syndication model that I personally benefited from because of my involvement with *90210* was now over. So I started to think about what would take its place, and created something called *Starbucks Presents*. What I basically said to Starbucks was, "You should create a social network based on your in-store relationships and have an in-store technology where people can be at their computers watching *Starbucks Presents*." And the fellows at Starbucks basically said to us at that point, and this was April 2006. "You know what, we're in the music business. Come back to us in five years."

But as traditional scripted network television, where Rosin had worked consistently for the past twenty years, continued to shrink, and the Internet continued to grow, Rosin pressed ahead and developed showbizzle.com. *Unfortunately, mainstream Hollywood lagged behind.*

BROWN: Well, the point you bring up that's interesting to me is that in the older TV business model, you were a creative person and you worked within a corporate structure. And now, being a creative person involves being not just an auteur but an entrepreneur.

ROSIN: Digital media is a huge threat to the status quo. I was represented by ICM when we made the first 30 episodes of *showbizzle*, and you go in there and they say, "OK, good. Where do you want us to sell this?" And I go, "I don't want you to sell it. I want to own it." The point about being in digital was you had ownership. Why pitch your ideas away when you can produce them yourself? But most of the mainstream players at that time were going, "Well, we're pitching it to MySpace." Or "We're pitching it to Sony's Crackle."

BROWN: They were still living in the old business model and they hadn't chosen to take advantage of the entrepreneurial opportunity to become the owner or the creative opportunity to be the final word creatively.

ROSIN: Well... yes. I benefited from the old business model when I was in my 30s, in the 1980s. Certainly, I don't begrudge anyone from doing that. But you find yourself not on the list anymore. I found the executives not very forthright. I found their comments not very interesting. Meanwhile my daughter, Lindsey Rosin, who I created *showbizzle* with, started winning playwright competitions. And seeing this and seeing my other daughter perform in high school,

I was overwhelmed by the level of talent I was seeing around by young people.

Showbizzle.com, both the website and the web series, continues to grow and evolve as Charles and Lindsey Rosin learn through hard-earned experience about the ins and outs of creating for the Web, building a site, and social networking. But the fact that they've been able to produce a high-quality product, pay all the actors, writers and crew for their services, and deliver all this at a cost of only $500 per finished minute is a testament to their creativity, ingenuity and skill.

BROWN: You've reached a very high level of success in mainstream television, and now you're working in the Internet. What's the most exciting thing to you about working in Internet television?

ROSIN: What's the most exciting? Being around young people, seeing them get their first opportunities. You know, so many of my colleagues who were veterans in television and had good careers in the network era sit around and bitch about the changes in our society and our business, and I understand those feelings and emotions. However, what attracted us to TV in the beginning, before we knew there was even a business that one could make a living at, was the opportunity to express ourselves creatively. The Internet gives us that opportunity in a way traditional TV never could.

BROWN: And it's great that you can combine the energy and enthusiasm of your daughter and her peers with and your experience and knowledge and wisdom and production savvy.

ROSIN: And I'm encouraged. This is the best time to be doing this because the mainstream media has not dominated original production for new media yet. They are still sorting out their finances, and all their problems. Independents can offer something that's different — like the show that Illeana Douglas is doing, having to do with her relationship with IKEA, or how Lisa Kudrow is doing something with Lexus. This is the wave of the future, and there's a viable audience out there. Whenever you read about new media they immediately say, "How are you going to get scale?" Well, scale doesn't really matter in the long run. What matters is finding a way for art and commerce to sustain themselves, which is what television had always been.

FRANK CHINDAMO

Mobile media master

Frank Chindamo is the creator and founder of Fun Little
Movies, a trailblazing company that develops, produces
and licenses original content
for global distribution on
mobile phones, the Internet
and portable devices. The
company's films have won
awards at the Cannes Film
Festival and the American
Cine Awards. Fun Little

Movies have played on networks worldwide including HBO,
Showtime, CBS, and Comedy Central. FLM's mobile comedy can
also be watched on Sprint, Verizon, Nokia, Motorola, AT&T and
iPhone mobile devices, as well as on the top Internet video platforms. Articles about the company have been featured in *Forbes*,
The New York Times, *Variety* and *Wired*.

Chindamo is a genuine pioneer in the field, creating and
licensing product for mobile distribution as early as 2004. FLM
now has distribution not only in the U.S., but in Asia, Africa, and
the Middle East.

BROWN: Frank, you were one of the pioneers in the field of creating
content specifically designed for the Internet and mobile devices.
How and when did you get into this?

CHINDAMO: Well, several years ago I was the bastard stepchild of the
cable networks. I had an office on Broadway in New York and we
would get a call from a cable outlet like HBO and they'd say, "We
need five 10-minute films," or "We need ten 2-minute films." They
were designed to be interstitial films that would go between the
feature films they aired. If the feature was 80 minutes long; they
needed another 10 minutes to get it to the 90-minute mark.

BROWN: Then the Internet came about?

CHINDAMO: Yes. The Internet. It's very popular. I think it's going to catch on.

BROWN: I suspect you're right, although I'm notoriously bad at predicting which technology will catch on. I worked on a commercial for IBM in the early '70s about this new thing they were developing for banks called an ATM. I distinctly remember thinking at the time, "Who the hell is going to use these things? You just trust they give you the right amount of money?" I'm not a good prognosticator. You're clearly better at this than I am.

CHINDAMO: Isn't prognostication something one does in Prague?

BROWN: So, how did you start creating for the Internet and for mobile platforms? Or did you do mobile stuff for phones first and then expand to the Internet?

CHINDAMO: Based on our experience making short films for cable, we got a contract with Warnerbros.com to create a series of shorts for their site. They commissioned us to do 26 of them. I moved out to L.A., bought a condo in the Hollywood Hills, and felt like, "Wow, this is great. I'm making loads of short movies for Warnerbros.com."

BROWN: In your mind, your career was set and you had made it big in Hollywood.

CHINDAMO: Yes. Then came the dot-com crash and suddenly the business of making these little shorts evaporated. I was reduced to working as an extra on movies. I even had mud poured on me on one scene. Symbolic of where my career had gone at the time, I guess. Anyway, I started to look around for other places to distribute short films and found a company that was putting shorts on pocket PCs back in 2003. Unfortunately, that was about as lucrative as selling star maps on Sunset Boulevard. Then, I finally got a break. I was contacted by the Cellular Technology Interactivity Alliance, a big convention that's held twice a year. And the keynote speakers that year were Bill Gates and Ted Turner.

BROWN: I've heard of them.

CHINDAMO: Then see if they'll give you a discount on my cable bill. They held up a mobile phone to the audience of 3,000 people and said, "This is the future — video on mobile phones." And it was our film.

BROWN: That's nice publicity.

CHINDAMO: It still took a long time for the form to catch on, but the publicity did get me known as one of the "go to" people in the world of short content for mobile devices.

BROWN: You both produce content and license it at Fun Little Movies. How do you find other producers whose content fits your brand and your business model?

CHINDAMO: Well, we have a very smart gentleman by the name of Matt Friedman who is our director of content acquisitions. Matt knows what we want, knows film really well and knows comedy. If you have content that you want to present to us, look on our website, there is a submit page.

BROWN: And are the submissions pilots or whole series? Or do people come in with a pitch?

CHINDAMO: It depends on who the person is. When an established screenwriter like Terry Rossio came in with a pitch created by Jocelyn Stamat for a series called *Turbo Dates*, we didn't need to see a pilot. We liked the idea and, based on his track record, had faith he could execute it perfectly. In fact, Jocelyn directed the winner of the 2009 Mofilm Grand Prize — a brand new Chevrolet!

BROWN: So for an established pro, you're willing to make a decision just based on a pitch. But for someone just breaking in...

CHINDAMO: If you're a person trying to break in and you haven't got any other assets or credibility besides a pitch, then no, a pitch is not good enough. You have to actually produce your idea and show it to us.

BROWN: It seems like the amount of short video content has exploded exponentially in the last two years.

CHINDAMO: Yes, it has.

BROWN: YouTube drives a lot of that for sure.

CHINDAMO: Right. But with YouTube it's important to keep in mind that 99% of the stuff is amateurish crap. It's open for anyone to post anything — there isn't any quality control.

BROWN: How many series have you produced and how many have you licensed?

CHINDAMO: As of today, we have about 120 series totaling about 1,600 actual films in the library and of that we produced less than half.

BROWN: When I went to your website I was impressed by how global your distribution is — you're in Asia, Europe, the Middle East, not just North America. Do consumer tastes differ greatly from continent to continent?

CHINDAMO: We found that physical humor is best, or character and situational humor as opposed to what most American sitcoms are based on, which is verbal humor and insult humor and pop culture jokes.

BROWN: So you either have to know the English language and/or American pop culture to get any of that.

CHINDAMO: Exactly. So we shy away from things that aren't universal and "evergreen," because if you send us something in March, we look at it in April, we send the contract in May, we get it up in June. It goes out to the carriers in July. They might then put it up in August and — poof — your "timely" joke is too old to work anymore.

BROWN: Sure.

CHINDAMO: So it's got to be evergreen, universal, and it has to be fairly positive in tone. Our mission is to spread love and laughter around the world. It can't be just bashing and negative. We don't do that.

BROWN: On your website you describe three basic streams of revenue, or "three buckets" as you call them. One is subscription, like you do with Sprint and other phone carriers. Next, there's pay-per-download, the iTunes model...

CHINDAMO: Which is dead as far as short videos are concerned.

BROWN: And bucket number three is advertising. Do you see advertising becoming the dominant revenue stream?

CHINDAMO: Well, yes and no. For now, advertisers are the main people with money willing to pay for the content in exchange for the chance to reach consumers with an ad before or after or beside the video. But it's still not an ideal way for the advertiser to reach the consumer with his message. So we're focused primarily on creating advertainment — entertainment combined with an advertising message embedded, hopefully naturally, within the storyline. We were the first to do it with a sitcom that took place at an Internet dating service as advertainment for a real Internet dating service called People to People. See *lovebytes.net*. Or better, a series for Planet Green called Bea Wildered that promotes the Planet Green TV channel and website with funny animated stories about a clueless environmentalist named Bea. Check it out at *planetgreen. discovery.com/videos/bea-wildered/*.

BROWN: Anheuser Busch tried this approach with the Internet channel BudTV.com. It didn't quite succeed for them the way they wanted it to, but I do think there is going to be more and more advertainment as you call it because people have so many ways to tune out traditional advertising and advertisers still want to get their message out there.

CHINDAMO: Several financial magazines did analyses of BudTV and said, "The one mistake they made was not hiring Fun Little Movies."

BROWN: They may be right. You specialize in comedies. In your opinion, is drama a tough sell on mobile platforms or the Internet?

CHINDAMO: All I've ever worked on is comedy. I started on *Saturday Night Live* and that's all we know how to do properly. Fortunately the five top genres in mobile entertainment are sports, news, weather, music and comedy. It's almost exactly like a newspaper — which, by the way, was the first form of mobile entertainment.

BROWN: Another potential growth area for short form content is as a development tool, a laboratory for networks to experiment with material. *The Simpsons* got developed that way originally — as one- or two-minute shorts that were part of *The Tracey Ullman Show*.

CHINDAMO: All the movies that were based on *Saturday Night Live* skits, the same thing.

BROWN: OK, the big question — what's the future? Where do you see all this going, say five years from now, all this meaning mobile content, short-form content. I realize that's a broad question, but give us a few thoughts.

CHINDAMO: Picture a triangle. It used to be a really thin, tall triangle with the most successful people at the top. If you were just trying to break in, it took a long time to get from the bottom all the way up to the top and you had to pass through a lot of gatekeepers and get an agent and slowly, slowly, work your way toward the top.

BROWN: That's the Hollywood Triangle.

CHINDAMO: That's the Hollywood Triangle, right? And now, it's as if the Internet just kind of sat on that triangle and now it's a really fat and broad at the bottom triangle where anyone, even a novice, can shoot his own video and post it on YouTube. As I said, there's a lot of crap on YouTube, but if you make something that's really good, you can go from the bottom of the triangle to the top a lot faster these days. Take, for example, the Felicia Day series called *The Guild*. It was shot in her apartment with $2,000 or $3,000 budgets and next thing you know it's winning the grand prize in NATPE and it's getting major financial support.

BROWN: I think the show is now in its third season and Felicia is selling DVDs of it all over the world. So an amazing story for her.

CHINDAMO: But she's not the only one. We were struggling before we won Mofilm, and now we're doing great. Making films used to be like sailing — you needed an expensive sailboat, training, etc., just to do it. Being on an Olympic sailing team probably meant you came from a background of enough money to buy a sailboat. But now, it's like basketball. Anyone with a ball can do it. Now in basketball, only the best succeed, and it's really hard to get to the pros, but all you need to start is a ball and a hoop. Internet filmmaking is a lot like that. You don't need expensive equipment and all that hoopla to succeed. Now you just need to be great at it, and the rest follows. My wife and I are writing a book on the subject as well, so if you like this book, you might like ours. Check out *funlittlemovies. com* for more info on that, or just to check out our films for a quick laugh. Thanks, Ross.

EPILOGUE
YOU'RE READY! HONEST! SO GO DO IT!

Listen carefully: I suspect you might hear a low roar in the distance. That growling, grumbling sound you hear is the insatiable hunger of the Internet for fresh, entertaining content. Every laptop and desktop computer in the world yearns for it. Cell phones crave it. iPhones and iPads demand it. The hunger for new video entertainment is global and grows exponentially 24 hours a day, 365 days a year. And the best news of all is that entry to this world is open not only to established professionals, but to anyone with a video camera and some imagination.

Somebody is going to make a great web series and maybe even a great deal of money satisfying this profound hunger. In fact, the desire for short-form video is so enormous that it will take thousands and thousands of creators to feed it.

You can be one of those creators. It will take inspiration and a lot of hard work, but what the heck — have you got something else you'd rather be doing than creating a little video world of your own and sharing it with millions on the Internet?

There are always so many things I want to tell my students in the final minutes of our final class session. *I hope you learned a lot. I hope you had fun. Write well. Write often. Be bold. Be creative. Believe in yourself.*

Take chances. Make movies. Make us laugh. Surprise us. Entertain us. Move us. It's the last week of class, and I know the students are already thinking about Christmas vacation, or about their summer plans. But I'm a teacher, so I desperately want to be wise and inspirational, to send my film and TV students off with a sense of purpose and determination to make their creative mark on the world. I want to leave them with something pithy, something memorable, the perfect few words that will inspire them for decades to come and motivate them to tell great stories and make great shows. But in the end, the truth is that the best advice I can give is this: JUST DO IT!

It is humbling and a bit disquieting to be a supposedly learned college professor and realize that the best wisdom I can impart is an advertising slogan. But it really does boil down to that. Thinking about creating a web series is only worthwhile if you actually sit down, develop the idea and the characters, devise a pilot story, write a script, shoot it and edit it... and then make more episodes.

This book, I hope, has given you a lot of helpful guidance about the process of making a web series. But process is only meaningful if you also put it into practice. We all have voices of procrastination and doubt in our heads. You know the ones I'm talking about — the ones that tell you not to dream, to second guess every idea you ever have. Set them aside. Believe in yourself. Don't worry about what "they" want out there. Create a show that YOU would want to see and have faith that there are thousands and thousands of others like you out there on the Internet who will also want to see it.

Turn on your computer and surf the Net. Check out a few web series. Nine out of ten times your reaction will be *I can do better than that*.

Yes, you can. But only if you sit down today and get to work creating. You're ready! Honest! So go do it!

I can't wait to see your show.

APPENDIX 1
SCREENPLAY FORMAT TUTORIAL

FADE IN:

EXT. DEADHEAD GUITARS/SAN FRANCISCO - DAY

Each scene has a <u>complete slug line</u> stating whether it is interior or exterior, giving a reasonably specific description of the location and indicating day or night, dusk or dawn.

The first time a location is used, provide the most detailed description in the heading. Once you've established that Deadhead Guitars is in San Francisco, drop the San Francisco.

If it's important for the audience to know immediately that it's in a specific city, make sure there is some identifying landmark (e.g., the Golden Gate Bridge) or else add this line:

TITLE: "SAN FRANCISCO"

after the slug line or somewhere in the text. You can also use a title to indicate the time period, LIKE THIS:

TITLE: 1966, THE SUMMER OF LOVE

Specifying the time period in the slug line is inappropriate.

EXT. GOLDEN GATE PARK - DAY

When you switch to a new location, use another slug line indicating this. If you're shifting emphasis to a new area within this location, you can use an abbreviated slug line (or, more properly, *shot)*, such as:

ANGLE ON REDWOOD TREE

A squirrel with an acorn in his mouth scurries up the trunk. Or:

NEAR BANDSTAND

A YOUNG WOMAN dances and sways to music that only she hears. Generally, avoid explicit camera references — keep them *implicit*. For example: "A lone tear trickles down her cheek" implies a close-up of the young woman's cheek — you don't have to specify CLOSEUP or CU of her cheek.

On those rare occasions where you *absolutely must* make a close-up explicit, it works like this:

CLOSE ON - HER CHEEK

as a lone tear trickles down it. Then you follow it up with:

BACK TO SCENE

She wipes it off and continues dancing.

INT. HAIGHT ASHBURY APARTMENT - DAY

Sometimes you will need a "time cut" within a scene. This is because every second of screen time must be accounted for in a script. For example, the following paragraph:

"Freedom Jones enters the apartment, rolls a joint, smokes it, then stares at a blank TV screen as he consumes an entire bag of Oreos."

is *not* acceptable screenwriting, since the

above may take an hour or more. Instead, choose moments to cut from and return to the scene. For example:

Freedom enters, immediately removes his Sears repairman uniform.

CLOSE ON - A JOINT

as Freedom rolls it with precision.

PULL BACK TO REVEAL

Freedom is now buck naked, sitting on the floor next to a bag of Oreos, smoking the last of the joint staring at a blank TV screen. You can also do a slug line such as:

SAME LOCATION - A SHORT TIME LATER

and then use some visual clue to suggest time passing — say the bag of Oreos now being empty.

The first time you refer to a character in the description, capitalize the entire name, like when JERRY GARCIA enters the guitar shop and we've not seen him before.

In all subsequent references, such as when Jerry Garcia crosses the room, he's in plain old upper and lower case. However, in dialogue, the character name is always in all-caps:

> JERRY GARCIA
> Anyway, it's in all-caps in the identifying line above.

> BOB WEIR
> Although if I were to call out to Jerry Garcia in my dialogue, the name would not be in all-caps.

> JERRY GARCIA
> Far out.

Sometimes you may want the audience to hear a character before seeing him/her, yet the character is in the scene, for instance appearing unexpectedly from behind a door. In such a case, put (O.S.) after the name:

                    JERRY GARCIA (O.S.)
          Dig this: O.S. is an abbreviation for
          off-screen.

Sometimes the audience can <u>hear</u> a character's thoughts or there is a narrator speaking to us who is not in the scene. In that case, the use of V.O. is appropriate:

                    AGING HIPPIE (V.O.)
          This is an abbreviation for Voice Over.
          Whoa, it's kind of like when I hear
          voices in my head.

Important sounds are also in all-caps, as when POLICE SIRENS APPROACH.

Always double space between the scene description and dialogue but single space within either a continuous dialogue or a continuous descriptive section.

If your scene description continues on to an entirely different subject, skip a line between sections. Use the spacing on the page to your advantage — for emphasis, pacing and rhythm. Try to make the experience of reading the script as close to the experience of watching a movie as possible.

Long paragraphs of description are difficult to read. If your paragraph is more than four or five lines long, edit it down or break it up into smaller paragraphs.

                    JANIS JOPLIN
                      (grinning)
          Hey man, that (grinning) above my
          dialogue is called a parenthetical

> description. Use parentheticals
> sparingly — like when the character's
> manner or expression might change the
> meaning of the line. But don't overuse
> them, that's a drag.
>   (drinks some whiskey)
> You can also break up dialogue with
> minor actions, especially those
> referring to the character speaking.
> But never put a parenthetical at the
> end of dialogue (here).

If Janis takes another slug of whiskey — which
is always a possibility — write it below the
dialogue in an action or descriptive line, like
this:

She takes another slug of whiskey.

                    JANIS JOPLIN
        Got it?

She takes another slug of whiskey.

Also, if the action you need to describe is more
substantial, bring the description fully to the
left margin. If the same character continues to
speak after the action has been described, place
a (cont'd) after the name:

                    JANIS JOPLIN (CONT'D)
        Okay?

EXT. FILLMORE WEST - NIGHT

Generally, there is no need to write "CUT TO:"
between scenes. It is assumed that we cut from
one scene to another unless specified otherwise.

There are occasions to give us FADE OUT: or
DISSOLVE TO: or other specific optical effects.
But most optical effects are decided upon in the
editing room so be sparing in the script stage.

—1.5"—► Set your left margin to 1.5", your right margin to 1". Indent dialogue 2.5" from the left side of the page, and 2" from the right side of the page.

——————————— 3.5" ——————————► BOB DYLAN
Character names are set at 3.5" from the left side of the page.
———————————3"   ——————► (toots harmonica)
Parentheticals — both beneath the
——— 2.5" ——————►character name and within dialogue —◄—————— 2" ——————►
are set at about 3" from the left side
of the page and 2.5" from the right
side of the page -   ◄——————————— 2.5" ——————►
                    (toots harmonica again, then
                    clears throat)
So that if you have a particularly long
parenthetical, it'll look like that.

Top and bottom margins are approximately 1". Skip 2 lines between the end of one scene and the slug line of the next. These are reasonably standard guidelines, though you can fudge things if your script is running too long or short.

The typical font is Courier 12 pt. This font resembles that of a typewriter. It dates from the time long ago when scripts were actually written on typewriters. There are two good reasons why you should not use one of the more attractive fonts that came with your computer:

1. The Courier font is still the standard in Hollywood, so if you don't use it your script will immediately seem odd and, quite likely, *amateur*;

2. It's much easier to judge how long a script will run if it uses the standard font rather than something exotic.

If dialogue breaks across a page, handle it like this:

> JERRY GARCIA
> Start the dialogue normally, man, then
> (MORE)

> JERRY GARCIA (CONT'D)
> when the page breaks, type that MORE
> as indicated, repeat the character name
> at the top of the next page and put
> the cont'd in. It's not rocket science,
> man.

One formatting approach to avoid at all costs is
centering character names and dialogue, as in:

> GINSBERG
> I saw the best minds of my generation
> destroyed by madness, starving
> hysterical naked.

> SURFER KID
> Gnarly.

INT./EXT. MERRY PRANKSTERS VW VAN - DAY

Some situations aren't quite interior or exterior
but some kind of combination. If we, the
audience, are inside the car with the characters
but the car is outside, the heading would be as
above. Just use common sense.

Page numbers are in the upper right corner and
do not have a period after them.

6. INT. FAIRMONT HOTEL - NIGHT   6

A "selling script" doesn't have numbered
scenes, but a "shooting" script does. Scenes
should be numbered both left and right and
the number *should* have a period after it to
help distinguish it from a page number. When
someone buys your script, put scene numbers in;
otherwise, don't bother.

The major factors in determining a technical

scene (one that needs a new slug line to distinguish it from the previous scene) are <u>location of camera</u> and <u>time of day</u>. There is a change in technical scenes if we cut from day to night at the same location. It is a new scene if we cut from one room to the next room in continuous time.

There is no change in technical scenes if the camera stays in one location but can see into another. If we stay with LENNY BRUCE in the living room while he shouts to a STRIPPER taking a shower in the bathroom, it's the same scene. If the camera moves into the bathroom, it is a new scene.

In terms of style, the basic idea is to give the briefest complete description possible that emphasizes what is important and de-emphasizes what is not. Clarity and economy are crucial, so it is best to limit your descriptions to what can be <u>seen and heard</u>.

Try to live by the rule: <u>every sentence is a shot</u>. And every shot should have a subject-predicate — something doing something. Audiences, including readers, will hook onto action.

For example, instead of listing the contents of a room, then describing a character enter, try describing the character entering and reveal the contents of the room as the character walks through it. We'll follow the character's action and won't even know the room is being described.

Scripts are still printed on one side of a piece of paper, rather than double-sided.

FADE OUT

APPENDIX 2
RECOMMENDED READING FOR MORE DETAILED DISCUSSIONS OF THE CRAFTS

A complete discussion of each and every skill needed to make a short pilot — writing, directing, cinematography, sound, editing, graphic effects, production management, online marketing strategies, on and on — would require thousands and thousands of pages of text and would defeat the purpose of this book; i.e., providing a concise guide to the basic creative issues involved in creating a short-form TV series for the Internet. Still, many of you will want deeper instruction that this one book can offer in one or more specific areas. Fortunately, there is ample literature and instruction available on each of the relevant crafts and skills you might need. Here is a short guide to some of the resources filmmakers and film school faculty have found most useful in areas you may want to explore in greater detail:

GENERAL VIDEO AND FILMMAKING

Digital Video Secrets by Tony Levelle
Digital Moviemaking 3.0 by Scott Billups

WRITING

Creating Characters by Marisa D'Vari

DIRECTING

Directing Actors by Judith Weston

Film Directing Shot By Shot: Visualizing From Concept to Screen by Steven D. Katz
First Time Director by Gil Bettman

CINEMATOGRAPHY

Master Shots: 100 Advanced Camera Techniques to Get an Expensive Look on Your Low-Budget Movie by Christopher Kenworthy

SOUND

Sound Design by David Sonnenschein (MWP)
The Sound Effects Bible by Ric Viers

EDITING

Cut By Cut: Editing Your Film or Video by Gael Chandler
The Technique of Film & Video Editing: History, Theory, and Practice by Ken Dancyger
In the Blink of an Eye by Walter Murch

PRODUCTION PLANNING

From Word to Image: Storyboarding and the Filmmaking Process by Marcie Begleiter
Film Production Management 101: Management & Coordination in a Digital Age by Deborah Patz

APPENDIX 3
SYLLABI AND COURSE OUTLINES FOR TEACHERS

At Dodge College of Film and Media Arts at Chapman University, where I teach, I have developed a two-semester sequence called Byte-Sized Television I and II. In the first semester, each student pitches a concept and characters for a short-form Internet TV series. They receive feedback from me, then pitch a pilot story, write a script, and revise it after workshopping it aloud in class. From the eighteen or twenty pilot scripts written, I select two to be filmed. I select a director, producer, cinematographer, editor and so on for each pilot and guide the students through pre-production. Each pilot is then shot on digital video, edited, and refined until it is ready to be posted on the Internet.

During the second semester, the students write and produce three more episodes of each series. We focus on not only find-ing additional stories within the premise, but on expanding and growing the series and characters. The students change jobs on each episode to give them a variety of experiences — although the writer/creator always serves as executive producer and the final creative word on all decisions, just as is the case in the pro-fessional world.

The following syllabi and course outlines are provided to give you a sense of how to organize the courses on a week-to-week basis.

CHAPMAN UNIVERSITY
DODGE COLLEGE OF FILM AND MEDIA ARTS
FTV 313 – BYTE-SIZED TELEVISION I
FALL 2009

Instructor: Ross Brown
Class Hours: Wednesday 4:00 - 6:50 p.m.

Course Description

An exploration of the creative and logistic challenges of creating a narrative episodic television series and generating episodes. Each student will create and write a pilot script for a 5- to 8-minute narrative TV series. 2 scripts will "go to pilot" and be produced by the writer/creator with other students functioning as crew. The produced pilots will "go to series" with the creator functioning as executive producer and supervising a writing staff in development of several episodic scripts to be shot the following semester in FTV 413. All produced pilots and episodes will be webcast.

REQUIRED TEXT

Epstein, Alex. *Crafty TV: Thinking Inside the Box*. New York: Owl Books, 2006.

Grading

Grading will evaluate creative content, grasp of the concepts, professional presentation and growth through the semester and be based as follows:

Pilot script 40%
Collaboration and contribution to filming of pilot 20%
Short analyses of web series 20%
Participation in class critiques, etc. 20%

COURSE SCHEDULE – FALL 2009

WEEK 1 – 9/2

INTRODUCTION TO COURSE

WEEK 2 – 9/9

PITCH CONCEPT/CHARACTERS

WEEK 3 – 9/16

REVISE CONCEPT/CHARACTERS & PITCH PILOT STORY

WEEK 4 – 9/23

WORKSHOP FIRST DRAFTS

WEEK 5 – 9/30

WORKSHOP FIRST DRAFTS

WEEK 6 – 10/7

WORKSHOP REVISED DRAFTS

INSTRUCTOR SELECTS 2 SCRIPTS THAT "GO TO PILOT"

WEEK 7 – 10/14

PREPRODUCTION & CASTING PLANNING
FORM 2 CREWS
ASSIGN JOB RESPONSIBILITIES

WEEK 8 – 10/21

PREPRODUCTION & CASTING
PROGRESS REPORTS FROM EACH JOB CATEGORY:

LOCATION AND CASTING UPDATE
PRODUCTION DESIGN REPORT
CAMERA/SOUND REPORT

WEEK 9 – 10/28

PREPRODUCTION & CASTING

FORMAL PRODUCTION MEETING ON EACH PILOT

DIRECTORS PRESENT PRELIMINARY SHOT LISTS

WEEK 10 – 11/4

FINAL PRODUCTION MEETING ON EACH PROJECT

DIRECTORS PRESENT REVISED SHOT LISTS

MAIN TITLE DISCUSSION ON EACH PROJECT

*** SHOOT PILOTS OVER WEEKEND 11/6 11/7 11/8 (2 CREWS)

WEEK 11 – 11/11

ROUGH CUTS

WEEK 12 – 11/18

FINE CUTS

WEEK 13 – 11/25

NO CLASS – THANKSGIVING HOLIDAY

WEEK 14 – 12/2

PITCH EPISODE IDEAS

WEEK 15 – 12/9

WORKSHOP FIRST DRAFTS

WEEK 16 – 12/16 (FINALS WEEK)

WORKSHOP REVISED FIRST DRAFTS

SCREEN PILOTS W/MAIN TITLES

CHAPMAN UNIVERSITY
DODGE COLLEGE OF FILM AND MEDIA ARTS
FTV 413/613 – BYTE-SIZED TELEVISION II
SPRING 2010

Instructor: Ross Brown – rbrown@chapman.edu – 714-744-2194
Class Hours: Wednesday 4:00 p.m. - 6:50 p.m.

Course Description

Building on the series pilots created in FTV 313, students will learn about the collaborative writing and production process as practiced in the creation of narrative episodic television series designed for the Internet.

Course Objectives

Course seeks to give students experience in working collaboratively on a narrative episodic television series designed for the Internet. Students will learn how each craft – writing, directing, on-set production, and postproduction – contributes to the overall vision and success of the series and of each individual episode. Students will also learn how each episode beyond the original pilot both tells a self-contained story and contributes to the overall ongoing story and growth of the series characters.

NOTE: THIS CLASS, DUE TO ITS NATURE AS A PRODUCTION COURSE, REQUIRES A LOT OF WORK OUTSIDE THE CLASSROOM. STUDENTS WILL BE ASKED TO WORK BOTH INDIVIDUALLY AND COLLABORATIVELY ON SEVERAL EPISODES AND TASKS SIMULTANEOUSLY.

Grading

Grading will evaluate creative content, grasp of the concepts, professional presentation and growth through the semester and be based as follows:

Written production analyses (Episodes 2, 3, and 4) 20%

Written final cut analyses (Episodes 2 and 3) 20%

Craft proficiency in your role(s) on each episode 30% (includes peer evaluation of your contribution)

Quality of your peer evaluations of others 20%

Participation in class critiques, etc. 10%

COURSE SCHEDULE – SPRING 2010

WEEK 1 – 2/3

INTRODUCTION TO COURSE - EXPECTATIONS
PRODUCTION PROCEDURES
SCREEN PILOTS
READ DRAFTS OF EPISODE 2
ASSIGN CREW ROLES AND INITIAL PREPRODUCTION TASKS
DISCUSS PRODUCTION NEEDS FOR EPISODE 2

WEEK 2 – 2/10

REWRITE/PREP EPISODE 2

PRODUCTION MEETING #1 – EPISODE 2

PAPERWORK TUTORIAL

WORKSHOP – CONTRIBUTING TO THE OVERALL CREATIVE VISION

STORY DISCUSSION – EPISODE 3 (ASSIGN WRITERS)

WEEK 3 – 2/17

REWRITE/PREP EPISODE 2

PRODUCTION UPDATE – EPISODE 2

READ ROUGH DRAFT – EPISODE 3

ASSIGN CREW JOBS – EPISODE 3

WEEK 4 – 2/24

REWRITE/PREP EPISODE 2

PRODUCTION UPDATE – EPISODE 2

LOCATION SURVEY – EPISODE 2

WEEK 5 – 3/3

FINAL PREP EPISODE 2

PRODUCTION MEETING #2 – EPISODE 2

READ EPISODE 3

PRODUCTION MEETING #1 – EPISODE 3

REVIEW SHOT LIST – EPISODE 2

ASSIGNMENT: WRITTEN PRODUCTION ANALYSIS OF EPISODE 2

SHOOT EPISODE 2 – FRIDAY 3/5, SATURDAY 3/6, SUNDAY 3/7

WEEK 6 – 3/10

SCREEN AND DISCUSS ROUGH CUT, EPISODE 2

PRODUCTION UPDATES – EPISODE 3

BRAINSTORMING SESSION – STORIES FOR EPISODE 4

WEEK 7 – 3/17

SCREEN AND DISCUSS 2ND CUT, EPISODE 2

REWRITE/PREP EPISODE 3

PRODUCTION UPDATES – EPISODE 3

WEEK 8 – 3/24

READ/PREP EPISODE 3

SCREEN AND DISCUSS 3rd CUT, EPISODE 2

LOCATION SURVEY – EPISODE 3

READ FIRST DRAFT – EPISODE 4

ASSIGNMENT: WRITTEN FINAL CUT ANALYSIS OF EPISODE 2

WEEK 9 – 3/31

SPRING BREAK

WEEK 10 – 4/7

FINAL PREP, EPISODE 3

REVIEW SHOT LIST – EPISODE 3

TABLE READ EPISODE 4

PRODUCTION MEETING – EPISODE 4

ASSIGNMENT: WRITTEN PRODUCTION ANALYSIS OF EPISODE 3

SHOOT EPISODE 3 – FRIDAY 4/9, SATURDAY 4/10, SUNDAY 4/11

WEEK 11 – 4/14

SCREEN AND DISCUSS ROUGH CUT, EPISODE 3

PRODUCTION MEETING – EPISODE 4

READ REVISED DRAFT EPISODE 4

WEEK 12 – 4/21

SCREEN AND DISCUSS 2ND CUT, EPISODE 3

READ REVISED DRAFT EPISODE 4

PREP EPISODE 4

DIRECTOR PRESENTS REVISED SHOT LIST EPISODE 3

WEEK 13 – 4/28

SCREEN AND DISCUSS 3RD CUT, EPISODE 3

PREP EPISODE 4

LOCATION SURVEY, EPISODE 4

ASSIGNMENT: WRITTEN FINAL CUT ANALYSIS OF EPISODE 3

SHOOT EPISODE 4 – FRIDAY 4/30, SATURDAY 5/1, SUNDAY 5/2

WEEK 14 – 5/5

FINAL PREP, EPISODE 4

REVIEW SHOT LIST – EPISODE 4

ASSIGNMENT: WRITTEN PRODUCTION ANALYSIS OF EPISODE 4

WEEK 15 – 5/12

SCREEN AND DISCUSS ROUGH CUT, EPISODE 4

FINALS WEEK – 5/19

SCREEN AND DISCUSS 2nd CUT, EPISODE 4

WRAP PARTY

ABOUT THE AUTHOR

Ross Brown began his writing career on NBC's award-winning comedy series *The Cosby Show*. He went on to write and produce such hit TV shows as *The Facts of Life*, *Who's the Boss?* and *Step By Step*. He has created primetime series for ABC, CBS and the WB. His play *Hindsight* received two staged readings at the Pasadena Playhouse (Pasadena, California) in July of 2007. His short play *Field of Vision* was performed in Chicago at the Appetite Theater's Bruschetta 2008 festival.

He is an Assistant Professor of Film and Media Arts at Chapman University in Orange, CA, where he developed a series of cutting-edge courses on creating TV series for the Internet. For updates to this book and the latest news and information on the world of web series, check out Ross's website at *www.bytesized.tv*.

THE WRITER'S JOURNEY
3RD EDITION

MYTHIC STRUCTURE FOR WRITERS

CHRISTOPHER VOGLER

BEST SELLER
OVER 170,000 COPIES SOLD!

See why this book has become an international best seller and a true classic. *The Writer's Journey* explores the powerful relationship between mythology and storytelling in a clear, concise style that's made it required reading for movie executives, screenwriters, playwrights, scholars, and fans of pop culture all over the world.

Both fiction and nonfiction writers will discover a set of useful myth-inspired storytelling paradigms (i.e., "The Hero's Journey") and step-by-step guidelines to plot and character development. Based on the work of Joseph Campbell, *The Writer's Journey* is a must for all writers interested in further developing their craft.

The updated and revised third edition provides new insights and observations from Vogler's ongoing work on mythology's influence on stories, movies, and man himself.

"This book is like having the smartest person in the story meeting come home with you and whisper what to do in your ear as you write a screenplay. Insight for insight, step for step, Chris Vogler takes us through the process of connecting theme to story and making a script come alive."
> – Lynda Obst, Producer, *Sleepless in Seattle, How to Lose a Guy in 10 Days;* Author, *Hello, He Lied*

"This is a book about the stories we write, and perhaps more importantly, the stories we live. It is the most influential work I have yet encountered on the art, nature, and the very purpose of storytelling."
> – Bruce Joel Rubin, Screenwriter, *Stuart Little 2, Deep Impact, Ghost, Jacob's Ladder*

CHRISTOPHER VOGLER is a veteran story consultant for major Hollywood film companies and a respected teacher of filmmakers and writers around the globe. He has influenced the stories of movies from *The Lion King* to *Fight Club* to *The Thin Red Line* and most recently wrote the first installment of *Ravenskull*, a Japanese-style manga or graphic novel. He is the executive producer of the feature film *P.S. Your Cat is Dead* and writer of the animated feature *Jester Till*.

$26.95 · 300 PAGES · ORDER NUMBER 76RLS · ISBN: 193290736x

MAKING IT BIG IN SHORTS
2ND EDITION
THE ULTIMATE FILMMAKER'S GUIDE TO SHORT FILMS

KIM ADELMAN

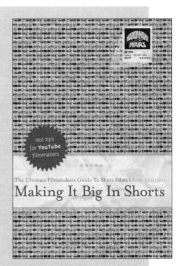

Grab a camera, make a short film. Show it at Sundance; show it on YouTube. There's no limit to what you can achieve by starting small and dreaming big.

In easy-to-follow steps, short-film guru, Kim Adelman, shows you how to achieve your dreams by making that killer short film. Bringing together the artistic and business sides of filmmaking, this book gives filmmakers the skills to develop unique shorts that are creatively satisfying and can launch careers.

This Second Edition of the best-selling *The Ultimate Filmmaker's Guide to Short Films* addresses new avenues for short filmmakers, including 48-hour filmmaking challenges, and new media opportunities such as YouTube, iTunes, and the iPhone.

If you want to make it big in short films, this is the book you need.

"Kim is the undisputed queen of the short-film world. No one has a better resume, better relationships, and more passion for this particular art form than she does, and her willingness to share this knowledge, especially the hard-won lessons, is inspiring."
–   Mark Stolaroff, Producer/Founder, No Budget Film School

"An essential guide for anybody who wants to make short films, which is great, because I love the short-film format. It's the best!"
        – Bill Plympton, Oscar-nominated Animator: *Guard Dog, I Married a*
          Strange Person, www.plymptoons.com

"A practical, down-to-earth, soup-to-nuts manual on getting the most out of the short-film experience – from succinct tips on all phases of production, to making the most out of the film festival experience, and beyond. A must-read for any filmmaker who values thorough advice delivered with energy, humor, and a sincere affection for the medium."
        – Christian Gaines, Director of Festivals, Withoutabox – a division of IMDb.com

Kim Adelman produced 19 short films that played at over 150 film festivals, worldwide, and won 30+ awards. She currently is the short-film correspondent for the acclaimed independent film news service indieWIRE. Additionally, Adelman teaches "Making and Marketing the Short Film" and "Low Budget Filmmaking" at UCLA Extension, and leads filmmaking workshops across the United States, Canada, and New Zealand.

$22.95 · 264 PAGES · ORDER NUMBER 128RLS · ISBN: 9781932907582

MASTER SHOTS

100 ADVANCED CAMERA TECHNIQUES TO GET AN EXPENSIVE LOOK ON YOUR LOW BUDGET MOVIE

CHRISTOPHER KENWORTHY

Master Shots gives filmmakers the techniques they need to execute complex, original shots on any budget. By using powerful master shots and well-executed moves, directors can develop a strong style and stand out from the crowd. Most low-budget movies look low-budget, because the director is forced to compromise at the last minute. *Master Shots* gives you so many powerful techniques that you'll be able to respond, even under pressure, and create knock-out shots. Even when the clock is ticking and the light is fading, the techniques in this book can rescue your film, and make every shot look like it cost a fortune.

Each technique is illustrated with samples from great feature films and computer-generated diagrams for absolute clarity.

Use the secrets of the master directors to give your film the look and feel of a multi-million-dollar movie. The set-ups, moves and methods of the greats are there for the taking, whatever your budget.

"*Master Shots gives every filmmaker out there the blow-by-blow setup required to pull off even the most difficult of setups found from indies to the big Hollywood blockbusters. It's like getting all of the magician's tricks in one book.*"
— Devin Watson, Producer, *The Cursed*

"*Though one needs to choose any addition to a film book library carefully, what with the current plethora of volumes on cinema,* Master Shots *is an essential addition to any worthwhile collection.*"
— Scott Essman, Publisher, *Directed By* Magazine

"*Christopher Kenworthy's book gives you a basic, no holds barred, no shot forgotten look at how films are made from the camera point of view. For anyone with a desire to understand how film is constructed — this book is for you.*"
— Matthew Terry, Screenwriter/Director, Columnist
www.hollywoodlitsales.com

Since 2000, CHRISTOPHER KENWORTHY has written, produced, and directed drama and comedy programs, along with many hours of commercial video, tv pilots, music videos, experimental projects, and short films. He's also produced and directed over 300 visual FX shots. In 2006 he directed the web-based Australian UFO Wave, which attracted many millions of viewers. Upcoming films for Kenworthy include *The Sickness* (2009) and *Glimpse* (2011).

$24.95 · 240 PAGES · ORDER NUMBER 91RLS · ISBN: 9781932907513

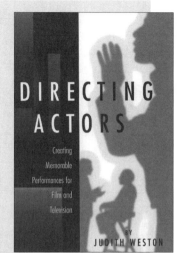

FILM DIRECTING: SHOT BY SHOT

VISUALIZING FROM CONCEPT TO SCREEN

STEVEN D. KATZ

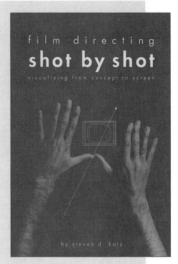

BEST SELLER
OVER 190,000 COPIES SOLD!

Film Directing: Shot by Shot — with its famous blue cover — is the best-known book on directing and a favorite of professional directors as an on-set quick reference guide.

This international bestseller is a complete catalog of visual techniques and their stylistic implications, enabling working filmmakers to expand their knowledge.

Contains in-depth information on shot composition, staging sequences, visualization tools, framing and composition techniques, camera movement, blocking tracking shots, script analysis, and much more.

Includes over 750 storyboards and illustrations, with never-before-published storyboards from Steven Spielberg's *Empire of the Sun*, Orson Welles' *Citizen Kane*, and Alfred Hitchcock's *The Birds*.

"(To become a director) you have to teach yourself what makes movies good and what makes them bad. John Singleton has been my mentor... he's the one who told me what movies to watch and to read Shot by Shot.*"*
        – Ice Cube, *New York Times*

"A generous number of photos and superb illustrations accompany each concept, many of the graphics being from Katz' own pen... Film Directing: Shot by Shot *is a feast for the eyes."*
        – *Videomaker* Magazine

"... demonstrates the visual techniques of filmmaking by defining the process whereby the director converts storyboards into photographed scenes."
        – *Back Stage Shoot*

"Contains an encyclopedic wealth of information."
        – *Millimeter* Magazine

STEVEN D. KATZ is also the author of *Film Directing: Cinematic Motion*.

$27.95 · 366 PAGES · ORDER NUMBER 7RLS · ISBN: 0-941188-10-8

THE MYTH OF MWP

In a dark time, a light bringer came along, leading the curious and the frustrated to clarity and empowerment. It took the well-guarded secrets out of the hands of the few and made them available to all. It spread a spirit of openness and creative freedom, and built a storehouse of knowledge dedicated to the betterment of the arts.

The essence of the Michael Wiese Productions (MWP) is empowering people who have the burning desire to express themselves creatively. We help them realize their dreams by putting the tools in their hands. We demystify the sometimes secretive worlds of screenwriting, directing, acting, producing, film financing, and other media crafts.

By doing so, we hope to bring forth a realization of 'conscious media' which we define as being positively charged, emphasizing hope and affirming positive values like trust, cooperation, self-empowerment, freedom, and love. Grounded in the deep roots of myth, it aims to be healing both for those who make the art and those who encounter it. It hopes to be transformative for people, opening doors to new possibilities and pulling back veils to reveal hidden worlds.

MWP has built a storehouse of knowledge unequaled in the world, for no other publisher has so many titles on the media arts. Please visit www.mwp.com where you will find many free resources and a 25% discount on our books. Sign up and become part of the wider creative community!

Onward and upward,

Michael Wiese
Publisher/Filmmaker

FILM & VIDEO BOOKS

SCREENWRITING | WRITING

And the Best Screenplay Goes to... | Dr. Linda Seger | $26.95
Archetypes for Writers | Jennifer Van Bergen | $22.95
Bali Brothers | Lacy Waltzman, Matthew Bishop, Michael Wiese | $12.95
Cinematic Storytelling | Jennifer Van Sijll | $24.95
Could It Be a Movie? | Christina Hamlett | $26.95
Creating Characters | Marisa D'Vari | $26.95
Crime Writer's Reference Guide, The | Martin Roth | $20.95
Deep Cinema | Mary Trainor-Brigham | $19.95
Elephant Bucks | Sheldon Bull | $24.95
Fast, Cheap & Written That Way | John Gaspard | $26.95
Hollywood Standard – 2nd Edition, The | Christopher Riley | $18.95
Horror Screenwriting | Devin Watson | $24.95
I Could've Written a Better Movie than That! | Derek Rydall | $26.95
Inner Drives | Pamela Jaye Smith | $26.95
Moral Premise, The | Stanley D. Williams, Ph.D. | $24.95
Myth and the Movies | Stuart Voytilla | $26.95
Power of the Dark Side, The | Pamela Jaye Smith | $22.95
Psychology for Screenwriters | William Indick, Ph.D. | $26.95
Reflections of the Shadow | Jeffrey Hirschberg | $26.95
Rewrite | Paul Chitlik | $16.95
Romancing the A-List | Christopher Keane | $18.95
Save the Cat! | Blake Snyder | $19.95
Save the Cat! Goes to the Movies | Blake Snyder | $24.95
Screenwriting 101 | Neill D. Hicks | $16.95
Screenwriting for Teens | Christina Hamlett | $18.95
Script-Selling Game, The | Kathie Fong Yoneda | $16.95
Stealing Fire From the Gods, 2nd Edition | James Bonnet | $26.95
Talk the Talk | Penny Penniston | $24.95
Way of Story, The | Catherine Ann Jones | $22.95
What Are You Laughing At? | Brad Schreiber | $19.95
Writer's Journey – 3rd Edition, The | Christopher Vogler | $26.95
Writer's Partner, The | Martin Roth | $24.95
Writing the Action Adventure Film | Neill D. Hicks | $14.95
Writing the Comedy Film | Stuart Voytilla & Scott Petri | $14.95
Writing the Killer Treatment | Michael Halperin | $14.95
Writing the Second Act | Michael Halperin | $19.95
Writing the Thriller Film | Neill D. Hicks | $14.95
Writing the TV Drama Series, 2nd Edition | Pamela Douglas | $26.95
Your Screenplay Sucks! | William M. Akers | $19.95

FILMMAKING

Film School | Richard D. Pepperman | $24.95
Power of Film, The | Howard Suber | $27.95

PITCHING

Perfect Pitch - 2nd Edition, The | Ken Rotcop | $19.95
Selling Your Story in 60 Seconds | Michael Hauge | $12.95

SHORTS

Filmmaking for Teens, 2nd Edition | Troy Lanier & Clay Nichols | $24.95
Making It Big in Shorts | Kim Adelman | $22.95

BUDGET | PRODUCTION MANAGEMENT

Film & Video Budgets, 5th Updated Edition | Deke Simon | $26.95
Film Production Management 101 | Deborah S. Patz | $39.95

DIRECTING | VISUALIZATION

Animation Unleashed | Ellen Besen | $26.95
Cinematography for Directors | Jacqueline Frost | $29.95
Citizen Kane Crash Course in Cinematography | David Worth | $19.95
Directing Actors | Judith Weston | $26.95
Directing Feature Films | Mark Travis | $26.95
Fast, Cheap & Under Control | John Gaspard | $26.95
Film Directing: Cinematic Motion, 2nd Edition | Steven D. Katz | $27.95
Film Directing: Shot by Shot | Steven D. Katz | $27.95
Film Director's Intuition, The | Judith Weston | $26.95
First Time Director | Gil Bettman | $27.95
From Word to Image, 2nd Edition | Marcie Begleiter | $26.95
I'll Be in My Trailer! | John Badham & Craig Modderno | $26.95
Master Shots | Christopher Kenworthy | $24.95
Setting Up Your Scenes | Richard D. Pepperman | $24.95
Setting Up Your Shots, 2nd Edition | Jeremy Vineyard | $22.95
Working Director, The | Charles Wilkinson | $22.95

DIGITAL | DOCUMENTARY | SPECIAL

Digital Filmmaking 101, 2nd Edition | Dale Newton & John Gaspard | $26.95
Digital Moviemaking 3.0 | Scott Billups | $24.95
Digital Video Secrets | Tony Levelle | $26.95
Greenscreen Made Easy | Jeremy Hanke & Michele Yamazaki | $19.95
Producing with Passion | Dorothy Fadiman & Tony Levelle | $22.95
Special Effects | Michael Slone | $31.95

EDITING

Cut by Cut | Gael Chandler | $35.95
Cut to the Chase | Bobbie O'Steen | $24.95
Eye is Quicker, The | Richard D. Pepperman | $27.95
Film Editing | Gael Chandler | $34.95
Invisible Cut, The | Bobbie O'Steen | $28.95

SOUND | DVD | CAREER

Complete DVD Book, The | Chris Gore & Paul J. Salamoff | $26.95
Costume Design 101, 2nd Edition | Richard La Motte | $24.95
Hitting Your Mark, 2nd Edition | Steve Carlson | $22.95
Sound Design | David Sonnenschein | $19.95
Sound Effects Bible, The | Ric Viers | $26.95
Storyboarding 101 | James Fraioli | $19.95
There's No Business Like Soul Business | Derek Rydall | $22.95
You Can Act! | D.W. Brown | $24.95

FINANCE | MARKETING | FUNDING

Art of Film Funding, The | Carole Lee Dean | $26.95
Bankroll | Tom Malloy | $26.95
Complete Independent Movie Marketing Handbook, The | Mark Steven Bosko | $39.95
Getting the Money | Jeremy Jusso | $26.95
Independent Film and Videomakers Guide - 2nd Edition, The | Michael Wiese | $29.95
Independent Film Distribution | Phil Hall | $26.95
Shaking the Money Tree, 3rd Edition | Morrie Warshawski | $26.95

MEDITATION | ART

Mandalas of Bali | Dewa Nyoman Batuan | $39.95

OUR FILMS

Dolphin Adventures: DVD | Michael Wiese and Hardy Jones | $24.95
Hardware Wars: DVD | Written and Directed by Ernie Fosselius | $14.95
On the Edge of a Dream | Michael Wiese | $16.95
Sacred Sites of the Dalai Lamas– DVD, The | Documentary by Michael Wiese | $24.95